TEACHER'S MANUAL

ENTRE CULTURAS

CROSS-CULTURAL MINI-DRAMAS FOR INTERMEDIATE THROUGH ADVANCED STUDENTS

BARBARA SNYDER

National Textbook Company
a division of NTC *Publishing Group* • Lincolnwood, Illinois USA

Contents

Suggestions for Classroom Use

PREPARATION

A. Collect and/or prepare all materials necessary. (Also, check the section titled on *Otras actividades*.)

B. You may want to make an advance assignment, such as asking students to do a report on the country discussed or an aspect of its culture, in order to help them understand the situation and context in which the cultural difference occurs.

C. You may want to review a pertinent section of the textbook, or another supplemental text that students have used, in order to help them relate the cultural difference to what they have previously learned.

INTRODUCTION

A. You may want to introduce and practice new vocabulary and usage, perhaps a day or two in advance. (You may also choose to prepare a brief gloss for them.) Check the *Vocabulario para repasar en adelante* section.

B. Introduce or review any grammar that the class may need in order to understand the conversation. Remember, however, that students reading for meaning can often capture the concept without resorting to detailed grammatical explanations.

C. Review the basic format of the capsules, if necessary. The characters whose names are in English represent American culture, and the characters with Spanish names represent the culture of a Spanish-speaking country.

D. If necessary, review the procedure of selecting answers and checking the follow-ups.

E. Just before presenting the culture capsule, ask the *Preguntas en adelante* questions and get several answers from various class members. This will serve as an advance organizer for the culture capsule.

PRESENTATION OF CAPSULE

A. Select from among the following alternatives:
  • The teacher may read aloud to the students.
  • The capsule may be read silently by each student, either in class or as homework.
  • The capsule may be read aloud by selecting a student from among the better oral readers.
  • The capsule may be read chorally by assigning sections of the class to each role.
  • The capsule may be read in small groups. The size of the group would depend on the number of roles. If there are two roles, have pairs of students read the

capsule to each other; if there are four roles, assign students to groups of four, with each student taking one role.

- The capsule may be dramatized by students who have prepared in advance to present it to the class. This may be a dramatic reading in front of the class, or may be memorized and presented as a skit.
- A tape of the conversation may be played. (Ask upper-level students to practice and tape it for lower-level students. Or, if native speakers are available, ask them to record it for you.)

B. You may, of course, choose more than one introductory activity. Some examples follow.

- The teacher may read the capsule to the class, and then have students read it in small groups.
- The capsule may be read silently by each student, and then read chorally by groups.
- The capsule may be dramatized in front of the class, and then read dramatically in small groups.
- A tape of the conversation may be played, and then individual student volunteers may read the roles.
- The capsule may be read in small groups, and then individual students (or several small groups) can read the roles for the class.

C. You may use one activity to introduce the capsule, then find the answer, and then use another introductory-type activity, so that it may be read with greater comprehension.

QUESTIONS AND POSSIBLE SOLUTIONS

A. Each individual student writes the answer that he or she has selected. The teacher may survey the students to see how many have selected each possible solution, and may then use the follow-ups by beginning with the solution least selected and proceeding to that most often selected, or vice versa.

B. A single student may volunteer an answer with an explanation of why that solution was chosen. The teacher should then use the corresponding follow-up. The teacher may want to call first on a student who did not select the correct answer, then select another student to give an answer. Again, the teacher may deliberately want to discuss a wrong answer. Proceed in this manner until calling on a student who selects the correct solution.

FOLLOW-UPS AND DISCUSSION

A. Read each follow-up until the correct one has been discovered.

B. Add any information desired, from either the Cultural Notes or from personal knowledge or experience.

C. Ask the *Preguntas después de leer* questions and get answers from several students in the class. The purpose of discussing the correct answer is to allow students to examine their own lives and culture, to encourage them to recognize differences in the way one views the world, and to present the opportunity for students to consider how they might deal with cultural differences.

ADDITIONAL ACTIVITIES

A. Students may write a continuation of the conversation in which the American character finally discovers the cultural difference.

B. Students may write a sequel to the capsule that takes place after the character has discovered the cultural difference.

C. Students may rewrite the conversation to portray a character who understands the problem.

D. If dramatization was not done in presenting the capsule, students may act it out afterwards. One method is to have a contest to see which group of students can best dramatize the capsule. The contest might include additional lines as suggested in Activity A or B.

E. Students may keep a cultural notebook in which they note examples of the cultural differences they have studied and add additional cultural items that they find in texts, newspapers, on television, or in meeting a Spanish-speaking person.

F. Students may do research to find additional information about the country or city in which the conversation takes place.

G. Students may be asked to plan a trip (such as a family vacation or a class trip) to the country or city in which the conversation takes place, or they may be asked to prepare travel brochures about the place.

H. Additional activities are suggested with each capsule. See the *Otras actividades* sections.

1 A sus órdenes

Preguntas en adelante:

1. ¿Qué expresión usas para saludar a un amigo en español? ¿a un desconocido?
2. ¿Dónde o en qué ocasiones conoces a personas nuevas?

Preguntas después de leer:

1. ¿Sabes la manera más cortés de presentar a personas que no se conocen?
2. ¿Qué acción hacen los uruguayos de todas edades al conocer a una persona nueva?

Notas culturales:

1. Many common expressions cannot be translated directly. *A sus órdenes*, for example, doesn't really mean that you should give someone orders. Another example is *Adiós,* which originated as the equivalent of "Go with God," and which is sometimes used instead of "Hello" when people pass each other on the street. When it is obvious that a literal translation does not explain how an expression is used, students should observe the situation or context for clues to meaning, or, if possible, ask someone who speaks both languages to explain.

2. A handshake is customary when meeting someone for the first time or when seeing an acquaintance again. But friends who see each other would probably use an *abrazo*. In this conversation, Ricardo and Teodoro certainly would hug each other, and Ricardo and Mateo probably would too. In Mexico, this applies to two men, two women, or to a man and a woman. In other countries, however, women kiss each other on the cheek when meeting. In Peru, for example, women kiss each other on both cheeks.

Otras actividades:

You might want to have students dramatize this conversation, using the correct gestures when meeting, and also to practice introducing each other, shaking hands and saying *a sus órdenes* after their names.

Suggestions for review:

Grammar review: forms of *estar*; forms of *ser*
Vocabulary review: courtesy expressions

Vocabulary

Vocabulario para repasar en adelante:

conocer—meet
hija—daughter
dale la mano—give him
your hand, shake hands
me divertí—I had a good
time, I enjoyed myself

cena—supper
dices: decir—say
vengan, viene: venir—
come
es hora de—it's time to

presentar—introduce
salúdale—greet him
quiero: querer—want
salir—leave

Additional vocabulary—Expresiones de cortesía:

¿Cómo está usted?—How are you? (formal)
Buenos días.—Good morning.
Encantado—delighted
Hasta entonces.—Until then. (specific time
or occasion)

Buenas tardes.—Good afternoon.
El gusto es mío.—The pleasure's mine.
Hasta más tarde.—See you later.
regular—okay, fair

Pequeño diccionario:

amigos—friends
años—years
aquí—here
bienvenido—welcome
buenas noches—good
evening
casa—house
cena—supper
comer—eat
comida—food
¿cómo están ustedes?—
How are you? (pl.)
¿cómo estás?—how are
you? (informal)
con—with
conocer—meet
conocerlo—meet you
creer—think
dale la mano—shake
hands, give him your hand
dices: decir—say
estado—state
Estados Unidos—United
States
estudiante de intercambio—
exchange student
excelente—excellent
familia—family
fue: ser—be

gracias—thank you
gusto—pleasure
hablar—talk
hasta—until
**hay: ¿qué hay de
nuevo?**—what's new?
hija—daughter
hora: es hora de—it's time
to
hoy—today
intercambio—exchange
invitarnos—invite us
jóvenes—young people
luego—then
mano, la—hand
mañana—tomorrow
más tarde—later
me divertí—I had a good
time
me llaman—they call me
mire—look
mucho gusto—(I'm) very
pleased (meet you)
muy bien—very well
nada: de nada—you're
welcome
nada de particular—
nothing in particular
niña—little girl

nuestro—ours
nuevo—new
órdenes, las—orders
pasa: ¿qué pasa?—what's
happening?
por—for
preciosa—lovely
presentar—introduce
presentarte–introduce you
pronto—soon
¿qué?—what?
quiero: querer—want
salir—leave
salúdale—greet him
señores–Mr. and Mrs.
sólo—only
tal: ¿qué tal?—how's it
going?
tarde: más tarde—later
tiene tres años—she's three
years old
tienes: tener—have
todo—everything
todos—everyone
vemos: nos vemos—we'll
see each other
vengan, viene: venir—
come

2 Bienvenidos

Preguntas en adelante:

1. ¿Qué hacemos para ser corteses cuando conocemos a alguien?
2. ¿Qué cosas crees que son muy descorteses?

Preguntas después de leer:

1. ¿Qúe nombre usan ustedes con sus vecinos y con los amigos de sus padres?
2. ¿De qué hablan ustedes inmediatamente después de conocer a una persona mayor por primera vez? ¿a una persona joven?
3. ¿Qué comen o toman ustedes que tiene el sabor de café?

Notas culturales:

1. Note the additional cultural information in Answer B.
2. See also Chapter 6, *Don Javier*, in this volume.
3. Bogotá is the capital of Colombia.
4. A custom that seems rather strange to Spanish speakers is asking about one's work. That is one of the first questions that an American asks after meeting someone, but it would probably not be asked by Spanish speakers. A Spanish speaker would more likely inquire about one's family and one's city.

Otras actividades:

Designate half the class as "adults" and half the class as "kids." To identify the "adults," use name tags or paper hats, have these students carry a book, or designate everyone not wearing jeans as an adult. Then, using a "party" format in which many pairs of students interact simultaneously, have students practice simple questions and answers, using the *usted* form and last name with those designated as "adults" and the *tú* form and first names with the "kids." (*¿Habla usted español? ¿Trabaja usted? ¿Dónde trabaja usted? ¿Prepara usted la pizza?*, etc.)

Suggestions for review:

Grammar review: gender (masculine/feminine forms); present tense
Vocabulary review: nationalities; courtesy expressions

Vocabulary

Vocabulario para repasar en adelante:

bienvenido—welcome
agregar—add
puente, el—bridge
esposo—husband

presentar—introduce
No se moleste.—Don't worry.
falta—lack

ingeniero—engineer
me acuerdo—I remember
mezclar—mix

Additional vocabulary: Las nacionalidades hispánias:

argentino—Argentinian
costarricense—Costa Rican
ecuatoriano—Ecuadorian
mexicano—Mexican
paraguayo—Paraguayan
salvadoreño—Salvadoran
venezolano—Venezuelan

boliviano—Bolivian
cubano—Cuban
guatemalteco—Guatemalan
nicaragüense—Nicaraguan
peruano—Peruvian
uruguayo—Uruguayan

chileno—Chilean
dominicano—Dominican
hondureño—Honduran
panameño—Panamanian
puertorriqueño—Puerto
  Rican

Pequeño diccionario:

agregar—add
ahora—now
allá—there
aquí—here
azúcar el—sugar
bastante—rather, quite
bienvenido—welcome
bueno—nice, good
café, el—coffee
casa—house
casi—almost
colombiano—Colombian
con—with
construcción—construction,
  building
cortesía—courtesy
creer—think, believe
cucharita—teaspoon
dar—give
desayuno—breakfast
dice: decir—say, tell
diferente—different
durante—during
en vez de—instead of
encantada—delighted
español, el—Spanish

esposo—husband
Estados Unidos—United
  States
estudiante—student
falta—lack
familia—family
fuerte—strong
gracias—thank you
gusto—pleasure
hablar—talk, speak
igualmente—equally
ingeniero—engineer
inglés, el—English
ingrediente, el—
  ingredient
intercambio—exchange
interesante—interesting
leche, la—milk
lo siento—I'm sorry
luego—then
mañana—tomorrow
más—more
más tarde—later
me acuerdo—I remember
menos—less
mezclar—mix

mío—mine
molestarse—worry
montaña—mountain
mucho—much, a lot
nada—nothing
norteamericano—American
oficina—office
padres—parents
para—for
parte, la—part
pena—sorrow
por—for
porque—because
preocupado—worried
preparar—prepare
presentar—introduce
primero—first
puente, el—bridge
respeto—respect
sabor, el—flavor
tener razón—be right
tomar—take, drink
trabajar—work
vacaciones, las—vacation
visitar—visit

3 Es de Venezuela

Preguntas en adelante:

1. ¿Hay estudiantes en esta escuela que son de otros países? ¿De dónde son?
2. ¿Tienes parientes que son de otro país?

Preguntas después de leer:

1. ¿De dónde es tu familia? ¿tus padres? ¿tus abuelos?
2. ¿De qué nacionalidad es tu apellido?

Notas culturales:

1. Just as not all people in Hispanic countries have Spanish last names, not all people who live in Hispanic countries speak Spanish. In addition to immigrant groups who speak their native languages, there are also many indigenous groups who speak pre-Columbian languages—Quechua in Peru, Guarani in Paraguay, Quiche in Guatemala, and Otomac and Nahuatl in Mexico.

2. In Mexico City, one gets an idea of all the nationality groups if one observes the school buses from the many private schools. A few of the many such schools are the *American School, Boston American School, Buckingham Instituto Inglés, Colegio España, Colegio Franco Español, Colegio Israelita de México, Colegio Italia, Colegio Suizo de México,* and *Instituto Canadiense de México.*

Otras actividades:

1. Take a survey to see how many nationalities are represented by the last names in the class. You also might want to ask about their mothers' maiden names.

2. If available, look at the social section of Hispanic newspapers and find family names that are not of Spanish origin.

Suggestions for review:

Grammar review: forms of *saber;* forms of *conocer*
Vocabulary review: adjectives of nationality, languages

Vocabulary

Vocabulario para repasar en adelante:

guapo—cute	**tener razón**—be right	**mayor**—older
polaco—Polish	**dijiste**—you said, you told	**se parecen**—they look alike
vivió—he lived	**todavía**—still	**segura**—sure
conocer—be acquainted with		

Additional vocabulary—Las nacionalidades:

africano—African
árabe—Arab
canadiense—Canadian
francés—French
israelí—Israeli
ruso—Russian

alemán—German
brasileño—Brazilian
chino—Chinese
inglés—English
italiano—Italian

australiano—Australian
británico—British
escocés—Scotch
irlandés—Irish
japonés—Japanese

Pequeño diccionario:

además—besides
adoptado—adopted
allí—there
año—year
apellido—last name
aquí—here
béisbol, el—baseball
clase, la—class
conozco: conocer—be
  acquainted with, know
creer—think, believe
chico—boy
dicen: decir—say, tell
dijiste: decir—say, tell
el español—Spanish

estudiante—student
estudiar—study
familia—family
guapo—cute
hablar—to talk, speak
hermano—brother
juegan: jugar—to play
llamarse—to be called,
  named
matemáticas—math
mayor—older
mirar—look
nuevo—new
padres—parents
parecerse—look like, look
  alike

pariente—relative
pasado—past, last
polaco—Polish
porque—because
razón, la—reason, (be)
  right
saber—know
sé: saber—know
segura—sure
solamente—only
todavía—still
venezolanos—Venezuelan
Venezuela—a country in
  South America
vivió: vivir—live

4 ¿Qué le llaman al bebé?

Preguntas en adelante:

1. ¿Tienes hermanitos? ¿primitos? ¿Te gustan sus nombres? ¿Te gusta tu propio nombre?
2. En los Estados Unidos, ¿quién decide el nombre de un bebé?

Preguntas después de leer:

1. ¿Cuál es tu nombre, al estilo español?
2. En los Estados Unidos, ¿bajo que circunstancias puede ser el apellido de un hijo diferente del apellido de sus padres?
3. ¿Cómo se decidieron tus padres en tu nombre?

Notas culturales:

1. Note the additional cultural information in Answer C.
2. Hispanics who have recently arrived in the United States often have problems with their "last" names. Teachers may call parents of their students by the wrong name, or assume that the child is from a divorced or single-parent family when that is not the case. Trying to find their names on an alphabetized computer list may also present problems. Radio and television announcers, who often use only a last name to identify a person in the news, sometimes use the wrong last name.
3. One kilo (one kilogram, or 1,000 grams) equals 2.2 pounds.
4. By international law, the mother's maiden name appears on all passports, including those of the United States.

Otras actividades:

1. Ask students to figure out names for their immediate family showing what the two last names would be in a Spanish-speaking country. You might also want to include grandparents, aunts and uncles, cousins, and nieces and nephews.
2. You might also want students to invent "silly" last names. Using famous names, for example, a student might state "My father's name is Clint Black and my mother's name is Margaret Chase Smith, so my name is (Bob) Black Smith." *(Mi papá se llama Clint Black, mi mamá se llama Margaret Chase Smith, y por eso yo me llamo Bob Black Smith.)* Or "My father is Billy Crystal, my mother is Lucille Ball, and I am (Jane) Crystal Ball." *(Mi papá es Billy Crystal, mi mamá es Lucille Ball, y yo soy Jane Crystal Ball.)*

3. Find out the weight of several famous people, such as football players or jockeys, recently arrived babies of famous persons, or any volunteers from the class. Have students figure out the weight in kilos.

Suggestions for review:

Grammar review: possessive pronouns and possession with *de*
Vocabulary review: ordinal numbers; names; name vocabulary

Vocabulary

Vocabulario para repasar en adelante:

carta—letter	**traer**—bring	**embarazada**—pregnant
dar a luz—to give birth	**pesar**—weigh	**apellido**—last name
esposa—wife	**casada**—married	**casarse**—get married
explicar—explain		

Additional vocabulary: Los números ordinales

tercero, tercer—third	**sexto**—sixth	**noveno**—ninth
cuarto—fourth	**séptimo**—seventh	**décimo**—tenth
quinto—fifth	**octavo**—eighth	

Pequeño diccionario:

amigo—friend	**Estados Unidos**—United States	**mirar**—look
antes de—before		**niño**—baby
apellido—last name	**explicarte**—explain to you	**nombre, el**—name
bebé—baby	**familia**—family	**noticias, las**—news
bonito—nice, pretty	**fue: ser**—be	**otro**—another
bueno—good, nice	**grande**—big	**papá**—dad
carta—letter	**hablar**—talk	**pasado**—last, past
casada—married	**hermano**—brother	**pesar**—weigh
casarse—get married	**hijo**—son	**primer**—first
con—with	**joven**—young	**profesora**—teacher
creer—think, believe	**kilo**—kilo (2.2 pounds)	**recibir**—receive
¿cuánto?—how much?	**llamar**—name, call	**recuerdas: recordar**—remember
dice: decir—say, tell	**llamarse**—be called, named	**segundo**—second
dio: dar a luz—give birth	**mamá**—mom	**traer**—bring
embarazada—pregnant	**más de**—more than	**una vez**—once
español, el—Spanish	**más joven**—younger	**verano que viene**—next summer
esposa—wife	**menor**—younger	**visitar**—visit
estaba: estar—be	**mes pasado**—last month	
	mexicano—Mexican	

5 Amigos, primos y novios

Preguntas en adelante:

1. ¿Tienes una familia grande? ¿Cuántos primos tienes?
2. ¿Quién es el mayor de tu familia?

Preguntas después de leer:

1. ¿Qué nombres en inglés son de muchachos o de muchachas?
2. ¿Por qué tienes tu nombre? ¿Es un nombre especial en tu familia?
3. ¿Qué nombres en inglés pueden parecer muy diferentes en otros países? ¿Conoces a alguien que tenga un nombre no muy común?

Notas culturales:

1. The only common name used for either boys or girls is Trinidad.
2. Girls sometimes have "boys' " names. Jesús, especially María Jesús, is very common, and so is José, especially María José. Mary Jo Fernández (the tennis player) is actually María José. The only common "girl's" name for boys is María, especially José María. The Mexican patriot José María Morelos and the Cuban poet José María Heredia are examples.
3. Like many other Hispanic names, Amparo, meaning "refuge" or "shelter", is a name with religious significance.

Otras actividades:

1. Ask students to bring snapshots of friends (all the better if they have unusual names). In pairs, have students describe their friends to each other.
2. Keep a list of famous Hispanics (Gloria Estefan, Aranxa Sánchez, Julio Iglesias, Steve Ballesteros). Are their names common? Typical? Is there an English version of the name? What do the names mean in English?

Suggestions for review:

Grammar review: verbs *tener* and *venir*; *saber* versus *conocer*; gender
Vocabulary review: family and friends; descriptions

Vocabulary

Vocabulario para repasar en adelante:

tener en común—have in common
bien parecido—good-looking
mayor—older

conocer—know, meet
Me tomas el pelo.—You're kidding me.
te apuesto—I bet you

Additional vocabulary—Descripciones:

alegre—cheerful
bajo—short
delgado—thin
gracioso—amusing, witty
hermoso—beautiful
mediano—medium
pelirroja—redhead
rubio—blonde
tímido—timid, shy

amable—kind
cómico—funny
elegante—elegant
gordo—fat
inteligente—intelligent
menor—younger
pesado—dull, tiring
serio—serious
torpe—awkward, clumsy

animado—lively, lots of
of fun
feo—ugly
grosero—rude, gross
linda—pretty
moreno—brunette,
brown-haired
simpático—nice

Pequeño diccionario:

abuelo—grandparent
ahora no—not now
alto—tall
amigo—friend
aniversario—anniversary
año—year
apuesto: apostar—bet
aquí—here
bailar—dance
claro—certainly
común—common
con—with
conozco: conocer—know,
meet
creer—think, believe
¿cuántos?—how many?
¿cuántos años?—how old?
dice: decir—say, tell
domingo—Sunday
empezar—begin
es decir—that is
escritorio—desk
estudiante—student
familia—family
fantástico—fantastic
fascinar—fascinate

fiesta—party
fin de semana, el—
weekend
foto, la—photo
grande—big
guapo—cute
hermano—brother
hijo—son
intercambio—exchange
invitarlas—invite them
joven—young person
llamar—call
mamá—mom
mayor que—older than
me tomas el pelo—you're
kidding me
mirar—look
momento—moment
muchachos—boys
ningunas—none, not any
niña—little girl
norteamericano—American
novia—girlfriend
novio—boyfriend
nuevo—new
otra vez—again

para—for, in order to
parecer—be like, look like
parecido: bien parecido—
good looking
pelo: tomar el pelo—be
kidding
porque—because
primo—cousin
probablemente—probably
rubio—blond
saber—know
si—if
solamente—only
teatro—theater
tener en comun—have in
common
tío—uncle
toda la familia—the entire
family
todavía no—not yet
todos—all, everyone
tomar el pelo—be kidding
universidad, la—university
viene, vienen: venir—come

6 Don Javier

Preguntas en adelante:

1. ¿Tienen tus padres algún amigo interesante?
2. ¿Qué expresiones usas cuando quieres ser cortés?

Preguntas después de leer:

1. ¿Cómo llamas a los amigos de tus padres? ¿Cómo llamas a tus vecinos (los de la edad de tus padres o mayores)?
2. Si tuviéramos la expresión cortés "don" en inglés,, ¿con quiénes emplearías este título?
3. ¿Qué títulos de cortesía tenemos en inglés?

Notas culturales:

1. See the additional cultural information in Answer D.
2. See Chapter 2, *Bienvenidos,* in this volume.
3. The feminine form of *don* is *doña: doña Bárbara, doña Amelia, doña Luisa,* etc.
4. Colombia is the world's leading producer of emeralds. The finest emeralds in the world come from mines near the cities of Muzo and Chivor.

Otras actividades:

You might want to have students practice making introductions as though they were all distinguished people. Have them use the *usted* form and *don* and *doña* before their first names.

Suggestions for review:

Grammar review: forms of *bueno*; *de* phrases *(son de Colombia, amigo de mis padres, el dueño de esta joyería, el apellido de Don Javier)*
Vocabulary review: jewels and jewelry; more courtesy expressions

Vocabulary

Vocabulario para repasar en adelante:

algo—something
esmeralda—emerald
poder—be able to
culpa—blame, fault

mientras—while
aunque—although
dueño—owner

casi—almost
brocha—brooch, pin
joyería—jewelry store

Additional vocabulary—La joyería:

pendiente, el—drop earring, pendant
arete, el—small earring
prendedor, el—pin, brooch, clasp
pulsera—bracelet
diamante, el—diamond
oro—gold

anillo—ring
cadena—chain
gemelos—cuff links
reloj, el—watch
perla—pearl
plata—silver

Pequeño diccionario:

abuela—grandmother
abuelo—grandfather
algo—something
amigo—friend
apellido—last name
aquí—here
aunque—although
bastante—rather, quite
Bogotá—capital city of Colombia
Brasil—Brazil
brocha—pin
buen, buenos—good
casi—almost
comprar—buy

culpa—blame, fault
día, el—day
dueño—owner
esmeralda—emerald
familia—family
gusto—pleasure
hay—there is, there are
joyería—jewelry store
llamar—call
mientras—while
mío, mía—mine
mirar—look
mucho—a lot
mujeres—women
norteamericano—American

para—for
perdonar—pardon
poder—be able to, can
preguntar—ask (a question)
probablemente—probably
problema, el—problem
si—if
siento: sentir—regret, to be sorry
tienda—store
todos—all, everyone
venir—come
viene: venir—come

7 Señor Licenciado

Preguntas en adelante:

1. ¿Sabes presentar a dos personas, una a la otra?
2. ¿En qué situaciones conoces a gente nueva?

Preguntas después de leer:

1. ¿Qué títulos de respeto empleamos en inglés?
2. ¿Qué información sobre una persona incluímos en una presentación?

Notas culturales:

1. The Sister Cities program between Taxco, Mexico, and Canoga Park, California, that is featured in this conversation is an actual exchange that has been thriving for many years.
2. Taxco is a city built on a mountainside near Cuernavaca, between Mexico City and Acapulco. Its colonial architecture is preserved by law, and it is the silver capital of Mexico. Silver is mined here and silver arts and crafts are produced here. Much of the world's fine silver jewelry comes from Taxco.
3. Yoli is a Mexican soft drink similar to Sprite.

Otras actividades:

1. Collect magazine and newspaper pictures representing various professions. Hand out one to each member of the class, and then have students practice introducing each other according to their professions: *señor Secretario, señora Tesorera, señorita Dentista,* etc.
2. You might want to find out if your city or town has a sister city. If not, find out what the sister state of your state is, since all states have one, although many of these programs are not very active.

Suggestions for review:

Grammar review: forms of *querer*; forms of *poder*
Vocabulary review: professions; courtesy expressions

Vocabulary

Vocabulario para repasar en adelante:

intercambio—exchange

traer—bring
esfuerzas—efforts
divertirse—enjoy oneself

de acuerdo—in agreement

hospedada—lodged,
staying with
presentar—introduce

laderas—mountainsides;
slopes
bienvenida—welcome
platicar—chat

Additional vocabulary—El empleo:

astronauta—astronaut
bombero—fire fighter
cartero—letter carrier
electricista—electrician
piloto—pilot
intérprete—interpreter
policía—police officer
veterinario—veterinarian
meteorologista—
meteorologist

vendedor—salesperson
camionero—truck driver
granjero—farmer
licenciado—lawyer
hombre de negocios—
businessman
banquero—banker
plomero—plumber
arquitecto—architect

dentista—dentist
carpintero—carpenter
comerciante—merchant,
storekeeper
ingeniero—engineer
mujer de negocios—
businesswoman
enfermero—nurse
médico—physician

Pequeño diccionario:

acuerdo—agreement
ahí—here
ahora—now
alegrarse—be glad
algo—something
amigo—friend
ándele—go ahead
aquí—here
aspecto—aspect
bienvenida—welcome
bonita—pretty
ciudad, la—city
con—with
divertirse—enjoy oneself
encantada—delighted
encantar—delight
esfuerzo—effort
gusto—pleasure
hablar—talk
hermana—sister
hijo—son

hospedada—lodged, staying
with
intercambio—exchange
jefe—head, leader
jóvenes—young people
ladera—mountainside, slope
listo—ready
llamarse—be named, called
mío—mine
molestarse—be bothered
montaña—mountain
muchísimo—very much
nada: de nada—you're
welcome
órdenes, las—orders
oye—hey, listen
padre—father
para—for
parecer—seem
perdonar—pardon
permiso—permission

permitir—let, allow
por—for, on
por favor—please
porque—because
presentar—introduce
preservado—preserved
programa, el—program
puedo: poder—be able to,
can
rato—while, short time
recepción, la—reception
refresco—refreshment
si—if
situada—situated
todo—all, everything
traer—bring
traigo: traer—bring
ven, viene: venir—come
ver—see
vistosa—showy

8 Hey, Mister!

Preguntas en adelante:

1. ¿Vas a un mercado o a un supermercado?
2. ¿Qué venden aquí en los mercados?

Preguntas después de leer:

1. ¿Qué es la descortesía en el supermercado o en una tienda?
2. ¿Te molestas cuando una persona no habla inglés muy bien?
3. ¿Qué hacen los vendedores aquí para atraer a los clientes?

Notas culturales:

1. Note the additional cultural information in Answers B and C.
2. See cultural note in Chapter 18, *La niñera*, for information on Guadalajara.
3. In spite of the verbal "advertising" done by vendors in the markets, on the streets, or even in front of stores, almost all vendors are just hardworking salespersons. Their English may not be culturally pleasing and they may be annoying, but when one stops to talk to them, they are nice people. They are usually very helpful and are willing to answer many questions. Americans must remember not to get annoyed and not to stereotype other cultures or people just because their behavior is different from ours.
4. *Señor* means both "sir" and "mister", and thus can be used alone or with last names. *Señora* and *señorita* follow the same pattern. In addition to meaning "ma'am", or "Mrs.", *señora* also means an older woman respected because of her age, even if she is not married. *Señorita* means "Miss", but also generally refers to a young woman, whether or not she is married. See Chapter 9, *Sí señorita*, in this volume.
5. Another cultural difference that students may notice in a market is the custom of bargaining. Tourists are often offered *un precio muy especial* or told *Le voy a ofrecer un descuento porque usted es estudiante / es miembro del Club Rotario / habla español / etc.* As with the use of English, this is done in an attempt to make a sale; the goods are not "hot," nor is the salesperson dishonest. Actually, the American who wants the item and is willing to make a counteroffer, and then bargains to arrive at a mutually satisfactory price, often gets a great buy.

Otras actividades:

1. Have students observe American behavior for a few days and decide which American behaviors might irritate people from other countries who are not used to American culture.

2. In small groups, have students list advantages and disadvantages of the Mexican system of shopping.

Suggestions for review:

Grammar review: uses of *estar:* 1) location *(Los puestos de guitarras están por ahí. / Creo que están en esa dirección;* 2) adjectives *(Estoy seguro / Estoy cansado de esto.)* Vocabulary review: clothing, personal items (wallets, purses, etc). (See also Chapter 11, *El regalo,* and Chapter 19, *Somos doce.*)

Vocabulary

Vocabulario y expresiones en adelante:

bolsa—purse	**cartera**—wallet	**cuero**—leather
encontrar—find	**faltar**—to lack, need	**puesto**—stand, stall
vámonos—let's go	**bien educado**—well-behaved	**Cada cosa tiene su lugar.**—Everything has its place.

Additional vocabulary—La ropa:

abrigo—coat	**blusa**—blouse	**bota**—boot
calcetines, los—socks	**camisa**—shirt	**camiseta, playera**—tee shirt
chaqueta—jacket	**falda**—skirt	**jeans, los**—jeans
gorra—cap	**impermeable**—raincoat	**pantalones, los**—pants, slacks
sombrero—hat	**suéter, el**—sweater	
sudadera—sweatshirt	**traje, el**—suit.	

Pequeño diccionario:

ahí—there	**falta**—lack, need	**poquito**—little
aquí—here	**Guadalajara**—name of city	**por ahí**—over there
artículo—article	**guitarra**—guitar	**porque**—because
así—that's how	**guste: gustar**—like	**puedes, puedo: poder**—be able to, can
bolsa—purse	**hablar**—talk	**puesto**—stand, stall
cada—each	**huarache**—sandal	**¡qué...!**—how...! what a ...!
cartera—wallet	**impresionante**—impressive	**querer**—want, wish
casi—almost	**inglés, el**—English	**seguro**—sure
comprar—buy	**interesante**—interesting	**si**—if
cortesía—courtesy	**libertad, la**—liberty	**tal**—such a
cosa—thing	**lugar, el**—place	**todos**—all
creer—think, believe	**mercado**—market	**turista**—tourist
cuero—leather	**mexicano**—Mexican	**vámonos**—let's go
definitivamente—definitely	**mirar**—look	**vendedor**—vendor, seller
dirección, la—direction	**molestarse**—be bothered	**ver**—see
educado—behaved	**otra**—another	**vienen: venir**—come
encontrar—meet, find	**para**—in order to	**zapato**—shoe
enorme—big	**poder**—be able to, can	

9 Sí, señorita

Preguntas en adelante:

1. ¿Qué títulos usamos aquí antes de los nombres?
2. ¿Qué es la cortesía?

Preguntas después de leer:

1. ¿Cuáles son ejemplos de la cortesía en los Estados Unidos?
2. ¿Viajan ustedes con su familia?
3. ¿Adónde van ustedes de vacaciones?
4. ¿Viaja de negocios alguien de tu familia?

Notas culturales:

1. See also Chapter 6, *Don Javier,* and Chapter 8, *Hey, Mister!,* in this volume.
2. Guatemala is the Central American country to the south of Mexico. Long before the Spanish conquest, this was the center of the Mayan civilization.
3. Antigua is a beautiful old colonial city that remains largely as it was after the great earthquake of 1773. Some buildings still lie in ruins from that earthquake. Prior to 1773, Antigua was the capital of Guatemala.
4. The most important Indian market in Guatemala is in Chichicastenango, and when the thousands of Indians gather, one can see the modern version of ancient Mayan culture. Incense burns on the church steps and the language spoken is Quiche.
5. Atitlán is a beautiful and very deep lake surrounded by four classic cone-shaped volcanoes. Indians in colorful traditional clothing live in small villages that dot the shores of the lake. Today it is the most popular vacation spot in Guatemala.
6. Tikal is the site of spectacular Mayan ruins in the jungle of the Petén area of the Yucatán peninsula. In this formerly remote area, however, the government has begun to explore for minerals and to develop a major tourist resort site.

Otras actividades:

1. You might want to take a survey to determine which of the sites mentioned in the conversation students would most like to visit.
2. Ask students to find information about some of the great earthquakes: Guatemala, 1773; Nicaragua, 1974; México, 1985.

Suggestions for review:

Grammar review: stem-changing verbs *(pensar, querer, preferir, sugerir, poder);* verb + infinitive
Vocabulary review: family; transportation; courtesy expressions

Vocabulary

Vocabulario para repasar en adelante:

¿En qué puedo servirle? How may I help you?	**negocios**—business	**país, el**—country
folleto—folder	**horario**—schedule	**sugiero: sugerir**—suggest

Additional vocabulary: La familia

abuela—grandmother	**abuelo**—grandfather
bisabuela—great-grandmother	**bisabuelo**—great-grandfather
bisnieto—great-grandchild	**cuñada**—sister-in-law
cuñado—brother-in-law	**madrastra**—stepmother
madrina—godmother	**nieto**—grandchild
padrastro—stepfather	**padrino**—godfather
padres—parents	**primo**—cousin
sobrina—niece	**sobrino**—nephew
suegra—mother-in-law	**suegro**—father-in-law
tía—aunt	**tío**—uncle

Pequeño diccionario:

agencia—agency	**día, el**—day	**lago**—lake
agente—agent	**e**—and	**lejos**—far
antes—before	**enseñarme**—show me	**lugares, los**—places
Antigua—a city in Guatemala	**esposo**—husband	**mañana**—tomorrow
aquí—here	**excelente**—excellent	**maya**—Mayan
Atitlán—a lake in Guatemala	**excursión, la**—excursion, trip	**mejor**—better
avión, el—airplane	**familia**—family	**negocios**—business
bonito—pretty	**folleto**—folder	**ni...ni**—neither...nor
bueno—good	**hablar**—talk	**oportunidad, la**—opportunity
buenos días—good morning	**hacer**—do, make, take (a trip)	**país, el**—country
carro—car	**hasta luego**—see you later	**para**—in order to
ciudad, la—city	**hasta mañana**—until tomorrow	**pasar**—spend time, pass through
claro—certainly	**hijos**—sons, children	**perdón**—pardon me
con—with	**histórico**—historic	**persona**—person
¿cuántas?—how many?	**horario**—schedule	**por**—through
Chichicastenango—a town in Guatemala	**hoy**—today	**prefieren: preferir**—prefer
divertirse—enjoy onself	**interesante**—interesting	**primero**—first
		próxima—next

puede, puedo: poder—be
 able to, can
regresar—return
reservaciones, las—
 reservations
ruinas—ruins
semana—week
servirle—serve you

si—if
sitio—place
suerte, la—luck
sugiero: sugerir—suggest
tarjeta—card
Tikal—a Mayan tourist site
 in Guatemala
tomar—take, make (a
 decision)

trabajando—working
turista—tourist
vacaciones, las—vacation
ver—see
viajar—travel
viaje, el—trip

10 Mi cachorro

Preguntas en adelante:

1. ¿Cómo se llama tu perro? ¿Cómo es tu perro?
2. ¿Te gustan los animales domésticos? ¿Cuál es tu favorito?

Preguntas después de leer:

1. ¿Tiene tu perro o tu gato un nombre apropiado en español?
2. ¿Por qué tiene tu animal su nombre?
3. ¿Qué hace tu animal que es similar a una persona? (Personification)
4. ¿Es parte de tu familia tu animal? Explica por qué.

Notas culturales:

1. See the additional cultural information in Answers B and C.
2. See also *Notas culturales,* Chapter 29, *En San Cristóbal,* in this volume.
3. Other animal vocabulary: animal skin is never *cutis,* no matter how soft, but *piel*; and noses of animals are usually *hocicos,* not *narices.* More idiomatic expressions: People are not "top dogs"; they triumph (*triunfar*); and people don't "go to the dogs"; they are ruined (*arruinarse*). If a person is "a lucky dog," *es un tipo con suerte*; and if the person is "a dead dog," *es una persona caída.* Every dog has his day? No, *a cada uno le llega su turno.* Let sleeping dogs lie? No, *deja lo bueno en paz.* Expressions for the cat lovers in class: the cat's meow, the cat's pajamas - *una persona (cosa, plan, etc.) excelente o notable;* to let the cat out of the bag - *revelar un secreto;* cat burglar - *balconero*; cat calls - *silbos, rechiflas.* Some permissible animal comparisons, however, are the following: *correr como una liebre* (to run like a rabbit), *tener una mirada de águila* (to have eagle eyes), and *ser un perro viejo* (to be experienced). Notice that these permissible expressions are all compliments to the human involved.
4. There are other American animal customs that many Hispanics find strange. They are often surprised that animals are allowed to live in the house, to sleep on the furniture, etc., and they are really surprised by the huge pet food industry. Although Hispanics often have real affection for their animals, they are still animals and are not treated as humans.

Suggestions for review:

Grammar review: 1) object pronouns. 2) reflexive pronouns; 3) stem-changing verbs; Vocabulary review: animals; parts of the body (See Chapter 28, *Es invierno, ¿sabes?*)

Vocabulary

Vocabulario para repasar en adelante:

cachorro—puppy
regazo—lap
pata—paw
suena: sonar—sound

rabo—tail
gafas—eyeglasses
subir—climb

cazar—hunt
se cayó—he fell
payaso—clown

Additional vocabulary—Los animales:

caballo—horse
cordero—lamb
gato—cat
pájaro—bird

cabra—goat
gallina—chicken, hen
oveja—sheep
toro—bull

cochino—pig
gallo—rooster
pato—duck
vaca—cow

Pequeño diccionario

ahora—now
algo—something
amor, el—love
aprender—learn
aquí—here
buen—good
cachorro—puppy
caerse—fall
casi—almost
cazar—hunt
claro—certainly
comer—eat
con—with
conocer—know
creer—think, believe
cuando—when
curioso—curious
chica—girl
darle—give him
decir—say, tell
divertido—fun, entertaining
ejemplo—example
entender—understand
España—Spain
español—Spanish
estudiante—student
estudiar—study

expresión—expression
familia—family
gafas—eyeglasses
grande—big
hablar—talk
hambre, el—hungry
hermanito—little brother
hermano—brother
intercambio—exchange
investigar—investigate
jugar—play
libro—book
llamar—call
llamarse—be named, called
llevara: llevar—wear,
  carry, take
mirar—look
montaña—mountain
nada—nothing, not at all
nadie—no one, nobody
nombrar—name
nombre, el—name
nuevo—new
oído—ear (inner part)
ojo—eye
oreja—ear (outer part)
otra vez—again

parecer—seem
pata—paw
payaso—clown
pequeño—small
perro—dog
pie—foot
piensas: pensar—think
pobre—poor
poner—put, place
por eso—therefore
porque—because
primer—first
profesor, el—professor,
  teacher
querer—want, wish, love
rabo—tail
regazo—lap
se cayó—he fell
sé: saber—know
simpático—nice
subir—climb, go up
suena: sonar—sound
todavía—still
todo—all
ver—see
viene: venir—come

11 El regalo

Preguntas en adelante:

1. ¿Qué clase de regalos te gusta recibir para tu cumpleaños?
2. ¿Cuáles son algunos regalos típicos que recibes?
3. ¿Quién te da los mejores regalos?
4. ¿Qué regalos te gusta darles a tus amigos para sus cumpleaños?

Preguntas después de leer:

1. ¿Qué tienes que es muy pequeño y que te gusta mucho?
2. ¿Tienes cosas de otros países? ¿Cuáles son? ¿Cómo son diferentes a las cosas de aquí?

Notas culturales:

1. Puebla, Mexico is a city southeast of Mexico City, on the other side of the two volcanoes, Popocatepetl and Ixtacchihuatl. It is located in a large and fertile valley. They say that there are so many churches in Puebla Valley that one could go to a different church every day of the year. There are many interesting tourist sites in Puebla, and most tourists also visit an onyx workshop and buy onyx souvenirs, such as bookends, figurines, tables, and candlesticks. Puebla is also noted for its Talavera tile and its pottery.

2. Many American students reside in the Puebla area, since the University of the Americas, which is accredited in the United States, is located in nearby Cholula.

3. Streets in Mexico are often named for famous dates. The two most common are Dieciséis de Septiembre (Mexican Independence Day) and Cinco de Mayo (Mexican defeat of the French at Puebla).

Otras actividades:

You may want to ask students to bring an item that they have from another country, or a very small item of some sort, and have a "Show and Tell" Day. First, put students in groups of four. Each of the four students tells the group about his or her item. The group decides (by vote) which is the most interesting item of the four. Then they tell the entire class about their items. Before speaking, however, have the students in the group help their spokesperson with any vocabulary or phrases he or she might need to do a good presentation.

Suggestions for review:

Grammar review: adjectives, diminutives (-ito, -ita). (See Chapter 20, Reina.)
Vocabulary review: gift items (See also Chapter 6, Don Javier; Chapter 8, Hey, Mister!; and Chapter 19, Somos doce.)

Vocabulary

Vocabulario para repasar en adelante:

regalito—little gift
caja—box
detalle, el—detail
tapa—cover
concha—shell

ábrelo—open it
cajita—little box
adentro—inside
ónix—onyx, a crystal-like
  stone

recuerdo—memento,
  souvenir
arete—earring
guardar—keep
anillo—ring

Additional vocabulary—Los regalos:

bolsa—purse
camisa—shirt
collar, el—necklace
joyería—jewelry
moño—bow
sudadera—sweatshirt
perfume, el—perfume

bufanda—scarf (winter)
cartera—wallet
corbata—tie
llavero—keychain
playera, camiseta—tee shirt
suéter, el—sweater.

calcetines, los—socks
cinturón, el—belt
disco compacto—compact
  disc
maquillaje, el—makeup
pañuelo—handkerchief,
  fashion scarf

Pequeño diccionario:

ábrelo—open it
adentro—inside
amable—nice
anillo—ring
aquí—here
arete, el—earring
bonito—pretty
buenos—good
caja—box
cajita—little box
comprar—buy
concha—shell
cosa—thing
creer—think
cumpleaños, el—birthday
delicado—delicate
detalle, el—detail
disco—record
¿dónde?—where?
dudar—doubt
escuchar—listen

Estados Unidos—United
  States
estampilla—stamp
extraños—strange
feliz—happy
figurita—little figure
guardar—keep
lo dudo—I doubt it
más tarde—later
mirar—look
muchas—many
muchas gracias—thank you
  very much
nada—nothing
nada más—just
norteamericano—American
nuevo—new
ónix, el—onyx
para—for
parecer—seem
pequeña—small, little

pequeñitos—very small
¿por qué?—why?
posiblemente—possibly
preciosa—precious
Puebla—city in Mexico
puedo: poder—be able to,
  can
razón: tener razón—be
  right
recuerdo—memento,
  souvenir
regalito—little gift
regalo—gift
sé: saber—know
siempre—always
tan—so
tapa—cover
tienda—store
traer—bring
ya—already

12   Malas notas, malas noticias

Preguntas en adelante:

1. ¿Son importantes las notas? ¿Por qué? ¿En qué clase recibes la mejor nota?
2. ¿Qué hacen tus papás cuando recibes una nota buena? ¿una nota mala?

Preguntas después de leer:

1. ¿Qué sistema de notas tiene esta escuela?
2. ¿Cuánto valen los exámenes finales?
3. Según tus padres, ¿qué es una nota buena?

Notas culturales:

1. In many Hispanic countries, grades in a course are based solely on a final examination. During the course, students are expected to complete the work on their own. There are no quizzes, no daily homework, and no projects. Neither are there report cards. At the end of the term, grades are posted publicly, either outside the classroom, outside the teacher's office, or on a central bulletin board.
2. Portillo is a large ski resort in the Andes mountains high above the city of Santiago, Chile. The best season for skiing is from May to September.

Otras actividades:

1. You might want to discuss the advantages and disadvantages of relying solely on an examination for a class grade.
2. Make a list of all the places where Chileans might go on vacation in their own country, and what activities they would do there. Where might people in Mexico or Argentina or Peru go on vacation?

Suggestions for review:

Grammar review: 1) reflexives: *preocuparse, alegrarse, divertirse, graduarse;* 2) ordinal numbers: *primero, segundo,* etc.
Vocabulary review: classes, numbers; letters

Vocabulary

Vocabulario para repasar en adelante:

nota—grade	noticias, las—news	No te preocupes.—Don't worry.
de todos modos—anyway	llevar—take	pegando—putting up
alivio—relief	idioma, el—language	podría—could
sacar una nota—get a grade	por ciento—percent	mejorar—improve

Additional vocabulary—Las clases:

alemán, el—German
biología—biology
comercio—business
computación—computer use
educación física, la—
  physical education
matemáticas, las—
  mathematics

arte, el—art
ciencias—science
mecanografía—typing
física—physics
geometría—geometry
estudios sociales—social
  studies

álgebra, el–algebra
ciencias domésticas—home
  economics
francés, el—French
historia—history
química—chemistry
lengua extranjera—foreign
  language

Pequeño diccionario:

además—besides, also
agotado—exhausted
ahora—now
algunas—some
alivio—relief
amables—kind, nice
año—year
aquí—here
bastante—rather, quite
bueno—good
clase, la—class
como—since, as
con—with
conmigo—with me
creer—believe
cuando—when
de todos modos—anyway
descansar—rest
después—after
difícil—difficult
Dios—God
divertirse—enjoy oneself
dormir—tsleep
durante—during
entonces—then
escuela—school
español, el—Spanish
especialmente—especially
esquiar—ski

**estudiante de
  intercambio**—exchange
  student
estudiar—study
exámenes, los—exams, tests
familia—family
graduarse—graduate
hacer—do, make
hola—hi
idioma, el—language
impresionar—impress
inglés, el—English
intercambio—exchange
literatura—literature
llevar—take
mal—bad
malas—bad
me alegro—I am glad
mejorar—improve
mío—my
mira: mirar—look
modos: de todos modos—
  anyway
muerto—dead
nota—grade
noticias, las—news
oye—hey, listen
para—for, in order to
pegando—putting up
poder—be able to, can

podría—could
por—by
por ciento—percent
Portillo—ski resort in Chile
preocupado—worried
preocuparse—be worried
primero—first
quiero: querer—want
resultados—results
sabes: saber—know
sacar una nota—get a
  grade
salir—come out, turn out
segundo—second
semana—week
semestre, el—semester
serio: en serio—seriously
sesenta—sixty
si—if
suerte, la—luck
sufrir—suffer
tener que—have to
terminar—end, finish
toda—all, whole
todos—all
vacaciones, las—vacation
viene: venir—come
verdad—right, true
vez: en vez de—instead of
vivir—live

13 Escuelas por todas partes

Preguntas en adelante:

1. Además de esta escuela, ¿a qué otras escuelas puedes asistir legalmente?
2. ¿Por qué asistes a esta escuela?

Preguntas después de leer:

1. ¿Qué clases necesitas estudiar para tu carrera?
2. Después de graduarse, ¿a qué escuela vas a asistir?
3. ¿Qué otras escuelas (de varios tipos) hay en los vecindarios cerca de esta escuela?

Notas culturales:

1. Note that the names of the schools mentioned are fictional.
2. Note that the following conversation (Chapter 14, *El colegio*) concerns the same family.
3. See the additional cultural information in Answer C.
4. Puerto Rico, of course, is a part of the United States and uses the typical American system of education.

Otras actividades:

1. If available, you might want students to check a phone book from a Mexican city to see what types of schools are available, and to compare them with schools in the United States.
2. You might want students to cite advantages and disadvantages of our system as compared to the Hispanic system. What reforms can students suggest to improve the American educational system?

Suggestions for review:

Grammar review: *asistir a*; *ir a*; adverbs (*bastante, tan, probablemente, solamente*)
Vocabulary review: upper-level courses; careers (see Chapter 7, *Señor Licenciado*); neighborhood vocabulary (to live, streets, neighbors, schools, etc.)

Vocabulary
Vocabulario para repasar en adelante:

triste—sad	asistir (a)—attend	vecindario—neighborhood
vecina—neighbor	ejecutiva—executive	solamente—only

Additional vocabulary—Clases avanzadas:

agricultura—agriculture
astronomía—astronomy
biología—biology
computación, la—computer
  use
física—physics
leyes, las—law
psicología—psychology
sociología—sociology
  teaching

anatomía—anatomy
álgebra, el—algebra
cálculo—calculus
contabilidad, la—accounting
estadística—statistics
geometría—geometry
pedagogía—pedagogy,
  teaching
zoología—zoology

arquitectura—archuitecture
bellas artes—fine arts
comercio—business
economía—economy
filosofía—philosophy
ingeniería—engineering
periodismo—journalism
química—chemistry

Pequeño diccionario:

academia–academy
aquí—here
asistir—attend
baile, el—dance
bastante—rather, quite
cerca—close
clase, la—class
colegio—school, high
  school
comercial—commercial
cuadra—block
diferentes—different
difícil—difficult, hard
educación física, la—
  physical education
ejecutiva—executive
empezar—begin
escuela—school
estudiar—study

gustar—like
hablar—talk
instituto—institute
joven—young
lejos—far
maestra—teacher
medicina—medicine
mexicanas—Mexican
mismo—same
muchachas—girls
Pacífico—Pacific (Ocean)
para—for, towards
parte—part
¿por qué?—why?
por todas partes—
  everywhere
prepa, la—preparatory
  school
preparar—prepare
primaria—primary (school)

probablemente—probably
públicas—public
quiere: querer—want, wish
secretaria—secretary
secundaria—secondary
  (school)
semana—week
semana que viene—next
  week
solamente—only
tan—so
todos—all
trabajo—work
triste—sad
turista—tourist
universidad, la—university
vecina—neighbor
vecindario—neighborhood
viene: venir—come
vivir—live

14 El colegio

Preguntas en adelante:

1. ¿Cómo se llama su escuela?
2. ¿Cuántos años vas a tener al graduarte?

Preguntas después de leer:

1. ¿Qué tipo de escuela es tu escuela? ¿Cuáles son las otras escuelas en tu distrito?
2. ¿A qué escuela piensas ir después de graduarte?

Notas culturales:

1. Note that the schools named are fictional.
2. Note that the preceding conversation (Chapter 13, *Escuelas por todas partes*) concerns the same family.
3. Other terms that may be used for high-school level schools are *preparatoria,* or *prepa; instituto*; and *academia.*
4. Among the attractions in Acapulco besides swimming are the water park, an amusement park, para-sailing, fishing, scuba diving, water skiing, boating, excursions to a tropical lagoon and a fort, shopping, and dancing. Many Canadians, Central Americans, and Japanese also visit Acapulco. Cici's is a very large water park in Acapulco.
5. Notice the switch from the polite form, *usted,* to the informal *tú* as soon as they introduce themselves. This is typical of the younger generation in Mexico.

Otras actividades:

1. Have students practice describing their school, their year in school, when they are going to graduate, etc.
2. You might want students to plan a trip to Mexico that includes Acapulco. Have them find out more information about Mexico City, Taxco, and Acapulco.

Suggestions for review:

Grammar review: stem-changing verbs (*querer, perder, poder*); *llamar* versus *llamarse; perder* versus *perderse; ¿cuánto?, ¿cuántos?*
Vocabulary review: time expressions (*tres días más, semana, el próximo año, el último año, ya);* months

Vocabulary

Vocabulario para repasar en adelante:

conocer—meet	costera—street along	perderse—get lost
cuadras—blocks	the coast	perder—lose
último—last	negocios—business	graduarse—graduate

Additional vocabulary: Expresiones del tiempo:

pasado: el año pasado—last year	estación, la—season	mes, el—month
un rato—a while	siempre—always	mucho tiempo—a long time
todavía—still	pronto—soon	
hace...(past)—Llegué hace una semana.—ago: I arrived a week ago.	hace ... (present):—Hace una semana que estamos aquí.—for: We have been here for a week.	nunca—never
		a veces—sometimes

Pequeño diccionario:

agua, el—water	escuela secundaria—secondary school	perder—lose
allí—there	estudiar—study	perderse—get lost
amigo—friend	graduarse—graduate	perdón—pardon me
año—year	gusto—pleasure	por—along
año que viene—next year	hermana—sister	puede, pueden: poder—be able to, can
aquí—here	inteligente—intelligent	
bastante—rather, quite	internacional—international	secundaria—secondary
centro—center	joven—young	semana—week
clase, el—class	junio—June	siga: seguir—follow, continue
con—with	llamar—to call	sólo—only
conocer—meet, know	llamarse—be called, named	tener ... años—be ... years old
costera—street along the coast	más de—more than	terminar—finish
cuadra—block	mexicanos—Mexicans	tiempo—time
¿cuánto tiempo?—how long?	muchachos—guys	todos—all, everyone
¿cuántos años?—how old?	mucho gusto—(I'm) very pleased (to meet you)	turista—tourist
de vacaciones—on vacation	nada—nothing	último—last
decir—say, tell	negocios—business	un poco—a little
día—day	niños—children	vacaciones, las—vacation
dirección—direction	padres, los—parents	ya—already
dónde—where	papá—dad	
	parque—park	

15   El club

Preguntas en adelante:

1. ¿Qué actividades tiene nuestra escuela? ¿En qué actividades de la escuela participas?

2. ¿Qué deportes tiene nuestra escuela? ¿Tiene esta escuela un equipo muy bueno? ¿Cuál es?

Preguntas después de leer:

1. ¿En qué actividades participas fuera de la escuela?

2. ¿Qué otras organizaciones tienen actividades para jóvenes de tu escuela? ¿la iglesia? ¿la ciudad o el pueblo?

Notas culturales:

1. Note: The names of the clubs are fictitious.

2. Cotopaxi, in the Andes Mountains forty miles south of Quito, is the world's highest active volcano, rising almost 20,000 feet above sea level. The last major eruption occurred in 1942.

3. Baron Alexander von Humboldt was a German scientist and geographer. (He founded modern geography.) From 1799 to 1804, he traveled extensively in Mexico, Central America, and South America, and because he publicized the natural wonders of Latin America in Europe, his fame is extensive in Hispanic countries. The cold Humboldt Current off the coast of Peru is named for him.

Otras actividades:

1. Have students prepare a list of all the activities and sports available in your school and write a short description of each. You might then want students to place them in order according to rank (or select the top five and the bottom five).

2. Then take a survey: If (because of finances, of course) all sports and activities at school were to be dropped except five, which five would your students keep? Or suppose that just five were to be eliminated. Which five would your students drop? Have each student prepare to defend his or her first and last choices.

3. You might also want students to list activities and sports that they participate in outside of school — through churches, clubs, friends, etc. Are there any activities that the school needs to add?

Suggestions for review:

Grammar review: shortened adjectives
Vocabulary review: sports; languages

Vocabulary

Vocabulario para repasar en adelante:

sobrevivir—survive
socio—member
natación, la—swimming
esquí, el—skiing

horario—schedule
escuela preparatoria—
  preparatory school
intramuros—intramurals

acostumbrarse—get
  accustomed, used to
alpinismo—mountain
  climbing

Additional vocabualry—Los deportes:

campo y pista—track
  and field
esquí acuático—waterskiing
buceo—scuba diving
gimnasia—gymnastics
patinaje artístico, el—figure
  skating
lucha libre—wrestling
jugador—player

equitación, la—horseback
  riding
fútbol americano, el—
  football
golf, el—golf
patinaje de ruedas, el—
  roller skating
voleibol, el—volleyball

atleta—athlete
boliche, el—bowling
boxeo—boxing
ciclismo—cycling
hockey, el—hockey
pesca—fishing
salto—diving
jai alai, el—jai alai

Pequeño diccionario:

académica—academic
acostumbrarse—get
  accustomed, used to
actividades, las—activities
además—also
alegrarse—be glad
algún—any
alpinismo—mountain
  climbing
allí—there
aquí—here
asistir—attend
aunque—although
basquetbol, el—basketball
bastante—rather, quite
béisbol, el—baseball
casa—house
cerca de—close to
ciencias—science
claro—certainly
clase, la—class
creer—think, believe
deber—should, ought to
dedicarse—be dedicated
deporte, el—sport
después de—after
diferente—different

difícil—difficult
domingo—Sunday
donde—where
entre—between
equipo—team
escuela—school
escuela preparatoria—
  preparatory school
español, el—Spanish
esquí, el—skiing
estadio—stadium
estudiante—student
favorito—favorite
fútbol, el—soccer
haber—have
horario—schedule
inglés, el—English
interesantes—interesting
intramuros—intramurals
juego: jugar—play
llevaba: llevar—take
menos: por lo menos—at
  least
montaña—mountain
natación, la—swimming
ningún—not any
noche, la—night

nombre, el—name
oficina—office
otras—other
participar—participate
partido—game
por eso—that's why
por lo menos—at least
posible—possible
primera—first
problema, el—problem
profesor, el—teacher
sé: saber—know
sean: ser—be
semana—week
sería: ser—would be
sobrevivir—survive
sociedad, la—society
socio—member
supuesto: por supuesto—of
  course
también—also
temporada—season, time
  period
tenis, el—tennis
tíos, los—aunt and uncle
ver—see
verdad—right

16   Las mañanitas

Preguntas en adelante:

1. ¿Tocas un instrumento musical? ¿cuál? ¿te gusta?
2. ¿Para qué razones tienes que levantarte temprano?

Preguntas después de leer:

1. ¿Qué cantamos aquí cuando es el cumpleaños de una persona? ¿Cuándo la cantamos?
2. ¿Qué clases de conjuntos hay? ¿Qué instrumentos usan?
3. ¿Qué canciones sabes en español? ¿Qué cantantes famosos cantan también en español?

Notas culturales:

1. See the additional cultural information in Answer C.
2. Young men often serenade a girl on her birthday or, more commonly, on her Saint's Day, or name day. This is called a *Día de Santo* and the expression that is equivalent to "Happy Birthday" is *Feliz Onomástico*. The name day for Ana, for example, is July 26.
3. The song *Las mañanitas* is sung by almost all Spanish speakers on special occasions: birthdays, saint's days, anniversaries, holidays, etc.
4. The custom of the Mexican mariachi originated in Guadalajara. The word "mariachi" originated with the French word for marriage. A traditional mariachi group has two guitars, a bass guitar, a trumpet, and a violin, but informally other combinations are common. Besides *Las mañanitas*, other common songs are *Guadalajara; Ay, Jalisco, no te rajes; La paloma; Adiós, Mariquita linda; Zacatecas; La negra;* and *Jarabe tapatío.*
5. In Mexico City, one can hire a mariachi group on the spur of the moment by going to Garibaldi Square, where there are always a few groups waiting. But almost all Mexican young people will know of a friend's mariachi group or play in one.
6. You might stop to listen to a mariachi group in a park or on the beach, but if you request a song, payment is expected, or at the very least a generous tip.
7. In some countries in South America, a serenade is followed by inviting the singers in for drinks and/or food, as we sometimes do with Christmas carollers here.

Otras actividades:

1. If there are a number of students who play instruments, have them form a mariachi, or have them get together as a group and learn a Mexican song or another song in Spanish.

2. Play *Las Mañanitas* each time a student has a birthday and by June they will know the song. Or you might want to have your students learn the words early in the year so they can sing it.

3. You might also want to play some of the classics listed in *Nota cultural 4*.

Suggestions for review:

Grammar review: verbs: *ir*; *tener*; *poder*
Vocabulary review: music vocabulary; days of the week; telling time

Vocabulary

Vocabulario para repasar en adelante:

tocar—to play music	**conjunto**—musical group	**guitarrón**—bass guitar
única—only	**canción**—song	**despertar**—wake up
levantarse—get up	**enojada**—angry	**saber**—know
entiendo: entender— understand		

Additional vocabulary—Los instrumentos musicales:

armónica—harmonica	**arpa**—harp	**banda**—band
clarinete—clarinet	**corneta**—cornet, bugle	**coro**—choir, chorus
flauta—flute	**harmónica**—harmonica	**marimba**—marimba
orquesta—orchestra	**oboe**—oboe	**órgano**—organ
piano—piano	**saxofón**—saxophone	**serenata**—serenade
tambores—drums	**trombón**—trombone	**tuba**—tuba
violincelo—cello	**xilófono**—xylophone	

Pequeño diccionario:

actividades—activities	**estudiante**—student	**mexicano**—Mexican
además de—besides	**formar**—form	**muchas**—many
algún—some	**grupo**—group	**música**—music
aprender—learn	**guitarras**—guitars	**para**—in order to
banda—band	**guitarrón**—bass guitar	**participar**—participate
canción—song	**hermano**—brother	**perfecto**—perfect
casa—house, home	**hoy**—today	**¿por qué?**—why?
con—with	**inglés, el**—English	**practicar**—practice
conjunto—musical group	**instrumento**—instrument	**puedo: poder**—can, be able
contrario—contrary	**levantarse**—get up	**saber**—know
creer—think, believe	**mañana**—morning, tomorrow	**salir**—turn out
despertar—wake up	**mañanitas**—early morning	**sábado**—Saturday
enojada—angry	**mariachi**—Mexican musical group	**sé: saber**—know
entiendo: entender— understand	**mayor**—older	**si**—if
escuela—school		**solamente**—only
		sólo—only

también—also

tan—so

tarde—late

temprano—early

tocar—play (music)

todavía—still

trompeta—trumpet

universidad—university

única—only

vámonos—let's go

verdad—right

17   ¿Qué llevas hoy?

Preguntas en adelante:

1. ¿A qué hora te levantas en la mañana y a qué hora sales para la escuela?
2. Por lo general, ¿qué ropa llevas cuando vas a la escuela?
3. Generalmente, ¿comes el desayuno en la mañana? ¿Qué tomas?

Preguntas después de leer:

1. ¿Llevas uniforme? ¿Por qué? (¿a la escuela, al trabajo, a jugar un deporte?)
2. ¿Cuáles son las ventajas de llevar uniforme? ¿las desventajas?

Notas culturales:

1. The school mentioned is fictional.
2. See additional cultural information in Answer B.
3. See *Encuentros culturales*, Chapter 25, *¿Qué usar?*
4. Alajuela is Costa Rica's third largest city. San José is the capital of Costa Rica.

Otras actividades:

1. Ask students to write short descriptions of uniforms (school, police, nurse's, etc.). With a partner, have them take turns reading their descriptions, with the partner trying to guess what kind of uniform they are describing.
2. You might want to ask students to design a uniform and describe it (purpose, items of clothing, color, etc.).

Suggestions for review:

Grammar review: reflexive verbs
Vocabulary review: clothes (See Chapter 8, *Hey, mister!*); time

Vocabulary

Vocabulario para repasar en adelante:

acostarse—go to bed	**pico**—little bit	**levantarnos**—get up
pelo—hair	**lavarme**—wash myself	**cuidar**—take care of
desayunarte—eat breakfast	**corto**—short	**permítame**—allow me
peinarme—comb	**maquillarme**—put on	**apúrense**—hurry
ponerse—put on	makeup	**llevar**—wear
cualquiera—whatever		

Additional vocabulary—Reflexivos personales:

afeitarse—shave
cepillarse—brush
dormirse—go to sleep
quitarse—take off

bañarse—take a bath
cortarse—cut oneself
ducharse—take a shower
secarse—dry off

cambiarse—change clothes
despertarse—wake up
lastimarse—hurt oneself
sentarse—sit down.

Pequeño diccionario:

academia—school, academy
acostarse—go to bed
apurarse—hurry
aquí—here
blusa—blouse
claro—certainly
clases, las—classes
como—as
corto—short
creer—think, believe
cualquier—whatever
cuidar—take care of
desayunarse—eat breakfast
desayuno—breakfast
difícil—difficult
Dios—God
día, el—day
escuela—school
estudiante—student
excelentes—excellent

falda—skirt
fácil—easy
hora—time
intercambio—exchange
jóvenes—young people
lavarse—wash
levantarse—get up
listo—ready
llamarse—be named
llevar—wear
mañana—tomorrow, morning
maquillarse—put on makeup
minutos—minutes
nada más—that's all
niñas—girls
pantalones, los—pants, slacks
peinarse—comb one's hair

pelo—hair
permitir—permit, allow
pico—little bit
ponerse—put on
porque—because
primer—first
profesores—teachers
puedes: poder—can, be able
públicas—public
quieras: querer—want
religiosa—religious
salir—leave
sólo—only
supuesto: por supuesto—of course
temprano—early
tengas: tener—have
terminar—finish
uniforme, el—uniform
verdad—right

18 La niñera

Preguntas en adelante:

1. ¿Tienes hermanitos? ¿Cómo son? Si no, ¿conoces a algunos niños?
2. ¿Ayudas a tus padres? ¿Qué haces?

Preguntas después de leer:

1. ¿A qué restaurante va más tu familia? ¿Quiénes van?
2. ¿A qué lugares va toda tu familia?
3. ¿Cómo se puede entretener a los niños cuando los cuidas?

Notas culturales

1. Note that the restaurant mentioned in this and the following two conversations is fictitious.
2. Note that the following two conversations (Chapter 19, *Somos doce,* and Chapter 20, *Reina*) concern the same family.
3. See additional cultural information in Answer B.
4. Day care-centers are not as common in the Hispanic world as in the United States, although in major cities where more and more women are entering the work force, a few are beginning to appear. Similarly, there are few rest homes and nursing homes. For the most part, family members figure out a way to care for one another within the family.

Otras actividades

1. If available, you might want to teach students a children's song so that they can reteach it to any children they babysit for. With this kind of logical rationale, most students will want to learn these "children's" songs.
2. For the same avowed purpose, you might also want to have students practice reading Spanish children's books aloud. Have students practice in small groups. Children's books in Spanish are now available in the exhibit booths of many state conferences and all major language conferences.

Suggestions for review:

Grammar review: *estar* expressions; subject pronouns; personal *a; tener* and its uses (*años, ganas, hambre, suerte,* etc.)
Vocabulary review: children (Sees Chapter 20, *Reina)*; numbers

Vocabulary

Vocabulario para repasar en adelante:

por supuesto—of course
cuidar—to care for,
   take care of

suerte—luck, lucky
supongo—I suppose
ayudar—to help

tener ganas—to be eager
debo—I ought to
vestir—to dress

Additional vocabulary—¿Cómo estás?

ocupado—busy
cansado—tired
mejor—better
triste—sad

preocupado—worried
contento—happy
nervioso—nervous
deprimido—depressed

aburrido—worried
enfermo—sick
encantado—delighted, pleased
enojado—angry

Pequeño diccionario:

¿a qué hora?—what time?
abuelita—grandma
adónde—where
ahora—now
allí—there
años—years
aquí—here
ayudar—help
bastante—enough
bueno, buenas—good
buscar—look for
casa—house
celebrar—celebrate
comer—eat
con—with
cuántos—how many
cubos—blocks
cuidar—care for, take care
   of
cumpleaños, el—birthday
deber—ought to, should
divertirse—enjoy oneself
domingo—Sunday

encantar—like very much
especialidades—specialties
esta noche—tonight
familia—family
fantástico—fantastic
fácil—easy
generalmente—generally
gracias—thanks
hablar—talk
hambre, el (f.)—hunger
hermano—brother
hoy—today
listas—ready
mamá—mother
media—half
mexicanas—Mexican
mientras—while
molestar—bother
muchachas—girls
muñeca—doll
niñera—babysitter
niños—children
noche, la—night

ocupado—busy
oigan—listen!
papá—father
para—for, to, in order to
pasar—happen
por supuesto—of course
probablemente—probably
pueden: poder—can, be
   able
restaurante, el—restaurant
río—river
salir—leave
sesenta y cuatro—sixty
   four
siempre—always
suponer—suppose
tiempo—time
toda—all
trabajar—work
vestir—dress
viejo—old
viene: venir—come
ya—already

19 Somos doce

Preguntas en adelante:

1. ¿Cuándo haces reservaciones?
2. ¿Por qué es necesario tener reservaciones?

Preguntas después:

1. ¿Sales para comer en restaurantes buenos? ¿Con quiénes vas? ¿Cuántos hay en el grupo?
2. ¿Cuál es un buen restaurante para los grupos grandes?
3. ¿Cuáles son los problemas especiales cuando hay grupos grandes?

Notas culturales:

1. See the additional cultural information in Answer C.
2. Note that the preceding conversation (Chapter 18, *La niñera*) and the following conversation (Chapter 20, *Reina*) all concern the same family.
3. See Chapter 39, *Es un buen precio*, in this volume.
4. Notice that Carol thinks that they will have a problem if they arrive "late." While this conversation concerns accommodations for large families in restaurants, another factor is also at work. Hispanics have a more informal view of time than we do, and are not compelled to do everything "on time," as most Americans are. Arriving half an hour late (by American standards) is well within the limit of tolerance by Latin American standards. (See *Encuentros culturales*, Chapter 16, *Una fiesta*.)

Otras actividades:

You might want students to role-play a family eating at a restaurant. Divide students into groups of seven — six in the family and one waiter. Start with their arrival and their seating at the table, then have them order a meal and chitchat while waiting for it. If possible, duplicate an authentic menu and have students order from it.

Suggestions for review:

Grammar review: Review of basic irregular verbs: *ir, tener, ser, estar*
Vocabulary review: clothes and colors (See also Chapter 8, *Hey Mister!*); family (See Chapter 9, *Sí, señorita*).

Vocabulary

Vocabulario en adelante:

abuelitos—grandparents
casi—almost
debemos—we ought
a tiempo—on time
ayudar—to help

regalito—little present
probablemente—probably
esperar—to wait
de veras—really

pañuelos—scarves
posiblemente—possibly
tendremos que—we will
  have to

Additional vocabulary—La ropa y los colores:

anaranjado—orange
castaño—brown
rosado—pink
cinturón, el—belt
enaguas, las—petticoat,
  half slip

azul—blue
gris—gray
verde—green
guantes, los—gloves
chaleco—vest
pijama, el—pajamas

blanco—white
morado—purple
corbata—tie
medias—hosiery
bata—robe

Pequeño diccionario:

a tiempo—on time
abuelita—grandma
abuelitos—grandparents
amarillo—yellow
amiga—friend
así—this way
ayudar—help
bastante—rather often
buen, buena, bueno—good
bonitos—pretty
casi—almost
collar, el—necklace
con—with
creer—believe,think
cumpleaños—birthday
dar—give
deber—ought to
definitivamente—definitely
difícil—difficult
doña—title of respect
dónde—where
encantar—like very much

encontrar—find
esperar—wait
grande—big
grupo—group
gustar—like
hora—hour, time
importar—be important
lista—ready
llegar—arrive
mejor—better
mesa—table
minutos—minutes
necesario—necessary
necesitar—need
niños—children
negros—black
ocasiones—occasions
pañuelos—scarves,
  handkerchiefs
para qué—for what
parecer—seem
pelo—hair

¿por qué?—why?
posiblemente—possiblement
probablemente—probably
problema, el—problem
querer—want, wish
regalito—little present
regalos—presents
reservaciones—reservations
restaurante, el—restaurant
rojo—red
segura—sure
sé: saber—know
si—if
tarde—late
tener que—have to
tiempo—time
tíos—aunt and uncle
traje: traer—bring
veras: de veras—really
vestido—dress
zapatos—shoes

20 Reina

Preguntas en adelante:

1. Cuando tu familia va a un restaurante, ¿cuántos van? ¿Quiénes son?
2. ¿Cuáles son los problemas especiales cuando hay niños con el grupo?

Preguntas después de leer:

1. ¿Tienes un apodo? ¿Es un nombre verdadero, o es inventado? ¿Por qué tienes este apodo?
2. ¿Quién en la clase tiene un nombre que es diferente de lo que le llaman ustedes?
3. ¿Cuáles son los apodos diferentes que usan tu familia y tus amigos? ¿Te gustan o no?

Notas culturales:

1. See also the cultural information in Answer A.
2. Notice that the preceding two conversations (Chapter 18, *La niñera,* and Chapter 19, *Somos doce*) concern the same family.
3. See also Chapter 48, *¿Quihúbole?,* in this volume.
4. Other common "names" used for young people: *Flaquito* and *Flaquita* (skinny), *Güero* or *Güera* (blonde), *Chato* and *Chata* (small nose), *Che* ("Mack"), and *Chulo* or *Chula* (cute and sassy).
5. The endings opposite of *-ito* and *-ita* are *-ón* and *-ona,* which mean "larger than normal", and which also sometimes mean "ugly" or "less than desirable": *sillón* (easy chair, arm chair); tazón—(large bowl, mug); *tablón*—(large board); *callejón*—(alley); *chipilón*—(crybaby, whiner); *soplón*—(tattletale, stool pigeon).

Otras actividades:

1. You might want to have students work in small groups to create the conversation as the family orders and eats their meal.
2. Ask students what nicknames they might give (in Spanish, of course) to Bibiana and Carol. What Spanish nicknames might various class members have? You also might want to list a few famous Hispanics and ask students to suggest the nicknames they might have had as children.

Suggestions for review:

Grammar review: *sentarse*; you might also want to practice nicknames to review *llamar* versus *llamarse: Me llamo Juan pero mi familia me llama Juanito.*

Vocabulary review: words that refer to babies and children; locative prepositions (See Chapter 35, *¿Dónde está el Focolare?*)

Vocabulary

Vocabulario para repasar en adelante:

tráiganos: traer—bring us
espérate: esperar—wait
sentados—seated
entre—between

más—plus
déjala: dejar—leave her
sentarse—sit
lado—side, beside

quédate: quedar—stay
vente: venir—come
durmiendo: dormir—sleep
llorar—cry

Additional vocabulary—Los niños:

bebé—baby
chiquis—little one
chiquitín, chiquitina—tiny baby, little tot
hijo—son
muchacha—girl
muchacho—boy

chiquito, chiquita—tot, toddler, little child
criatura—baby, child
hermanita—little sister
hermanito—little brother
nena—baby girl
nene—baby boy

chiquillo, chiquilín—child, rowdy youngster
hija—daughter
moza—young woman
mozo—young man
niñita—toddler girl
niñito—toddler boy

Pequeño diccionario:

abuelita—grandma
ahorita—right now
allí—there
aquí—here
bebita—baby girl
camarero—waiter
cerca de—close to
chiquillo—little boy
cochecito—baby carriage
con—with
conmigo—with me
cuántos—how many
dejar—leave
durmiendo: dormir—sleep
enfrente—in front, facing
entrar—enter
entre—between
esperarse—wait
familia—family
favorcito—little favor

gordito—chubby
hambre—hunger, hungry
hermana—sister
ladito—right beside
lado—side, beside
llegar—arrive
llorar—cry
más—plus
mesa—table
mi'ja: mi hija—my daughter
mirar—look
momentito—moment
nena—baby girl
niña—little girl
niño—little boy
niños—children
otro—other
oye—hey
pasar: ¿qué te pasa?—What's wrong

plato—plate
por favorcito—pretty please
¿por qué?—why?
precioso—precious, sweetheart
prontito—very soon
quedarse—stay, remain
reina—queen
restaurante—restaurant
sentados—seated
sientes: sentarse—sit down
silla—chair
taquitos—small tacos
todos—everyone
tráiganos: traer—bring
ven, vente: venir—come
ventanas—windows
verdad—right

21 Pido la pizza

Preguntas en adelante:

1. ¿Te gusta la comida de otros países?
2. ¿Qué comidas comemos que son de otro país originalmente?

Preguntas después de leer:

1. ¿Cómo te gusta la pizza? ¿Qué ingredientes tiene?
2. ¿Te gusta el arroz? ¿los camarones? ¿la salchicha?
3. ¿Qué comidas internacionales te gustan?

Notas culturales:

1. See Chapter 22, *¡Cuánta comida!,* and Chapter 23, *Enchiladas verdes,* in this volume.
2. When meats are used, rather than seafood, it is sometimes called *paella ranchera.*
3. The vocabulary group that differs most from one Hispanic country to another is food vocabulary. Just a few examples: *gambas* or *camarones* (shrimp); *salchicha* or *chorizo* (sausage); *melocotones* or *duraznos* (peaches); *toronjas* or *pomelos* (grapefruit); *remolachas* or *betabeles* (beets); *guisantes* or *chícharos* (peas); *judías verdes, habichuelas,* or *ejotes* (green beans); *legumbres, verduras* or *vegetales* (vegetables).

Otras actividades:

1. You might want to find a recipe and/or picture of paella, gazpacho, etc., before reading this chapter.
2. You might want to have a "cultural food" day. Give extra credit to students who really prepare a Spanish recipe (but not those who just bring chips and dip).

Suggestions for review:

Grammar review: negatives
Vocabulary review: snack food

Vocabulary

Vocabulario y expresiones en adelante:

entender—to understand	**hecha**—made (from hacer)	**camarones, los**—shrimp
servir—to serve	**mariscos**—seafood	**salchicha**—sausage
legumbres, las—vegetables	**pedir**—order	

Additional vocabulary—Bocadillos:

cacahuetes, los—peanuts
chicle, el—gum
palomitas—popcorn
paletas—popsicles
pasteles, los—pastry
sándwich, el—sandwich

caramelos—caramels
confites, dulces—candy
galletas—cookies
papas fritas—potato chips
pudín, el—pudding

chocolate, el—chocolate
helado—ice cream
refrescos, gaseosas—soft
  drinks
pirulíes, los—lollipops

Pequeño diccionario:

aquí—here
arroz, el—rice
buena—good
caldo—broth
camarón, el—shrimp
clara—clear
comida—food
con—with
costa—coast, coastline
diferente—different
entiendo: entender—
  understand
española—Spanish
especializarse—specialize
esperar—expect
Estados Unidos—United
  States
fría—cold

gambas—large shrimp
gazpacho—soup
gente, la—people
gigante—giant, large
hambre, el (f.)—hunger
hamburguesas—hamburgers
legumbres, las—vegetables
mariscos—seafood
mesa—table
mirar—look
nada—nothing
ni ... ni—neither, not ...nor
norteamericanas—
  American
pido: pedir—ask for, order
por eso—that's why
por fortuna—fortunately
porque—because

preparada—prepared
probablemente—probably
¿qué importa?—what's the
  difference?
restaurante, el—restaurante
rosbif, el—roast beef
sabrosa—delicious, tasty
salchicha—sausage
sirven: servir—serve
siempre—always
sopa—soup
tanta—so much
tener hambre—be hungry
tiene: tener—have, be ...
tomate, el—tomato
Valencia—una ciudad en
  España

22 ¡Cuánta comida!

Preguntas en adelante:

1. ¿Qué sopa te gusta más?
2. ¿Cuál es tu legumbre favorita? ¿tu postre favorito?

Preguntas después de leer:

1. ¿Hay dos palabras diferentes en inglés para hablar de la misma comida (por ejemplo, *wieners* y *hot dogs*)?
2. ¿Comes mucho la sopa seca, o pasta? ¿Cuál es tu receta favorita?

Notas culturales:

1. See additional cultural information in Answer B.
2. See Chapter 21, *Pido la pizza,* and Chapter 23, *Enchiladas verdes,* in this volume.
3. Americans often think that Mexicans eat too much, partly because their main meal is in the middle of the day, and partly because there are more successive courses. And Mexicans often think that Americans don't eat enough, because they think most Americans are too thin. The ideal weight for Mexicans is 10 to 20 percent more than it would be here.
4. The midday meal is traditionally composed of five or six courses: soup, pasta, salad, meat and vegetables, dessert, and coffee. Portions, however, are smaller than in an American meal of fewer courses, so unless one requests second helpings, overeating is not a big problem.
5. *Flan* is a custard made with a caramel sauce on the bottom. When turned out of the dish, the caramel sauce is on top and drips down the side. Even those who customarily don't like custard usually like Mexican *flan.*
6. Many exchange programs involving Latin American families are true exchanges: a family who sends a young person to the United States also receives a student. The American host families of these exchange students are, therefore, often upper middle-class families who have maids, cooks, and other help. The wages for these household servants is extremely low.

Otras actividades:

1. Bring recipes written in Spanish. Let students guess the product from reading the ingredients.
2. You might want to have a *sopa seca* day in class. Allow students to bring in a casserole of their favorite pasta dish.
3. You also could take a survey and ask students about unusual ethnic foods in their families and/or have an ethnic food day.

Suggestions for review:

Grammar review: *de* between nouns (*sopa de zanahorias*); indirect object pronouns with *gustar*
Vocabulary review: food

Vocabulary

Vocabulario para repasar en adelante:

comida—food
zanahorias—carrots
legumbres, las—vegetables
mezcla—mixture
sopera—soup tureen
escoger—choose

ganar—gain
lechuga—lettuce
postre, el—dessert
guisantes, los—peas
queso—cheese
entiendo: entender—
  understand

peso—weight
chuletas—chops
leche, la—milk
champiñones, los—
  mushrooms

Additional vocabulary—La comida:

plátanos—bananas
filete, el—steak
pollo—chicken
mantequilla—butter
mayonesa—mayonnaise
queso—cheese
manzanas—apples

camarones, los—shrimp
frijoles, los—beans
uvas—grapes
helado—ice cream
naranjas—oranges
fresas—strawberries
arroz, el—rice

puerco—pork
jamón, el—ham
galletas—cookies
huevos—eggs
pescado—fish
tocino—bacon

Pequeño diccionario:

año—year
aquí—here
buena—good
champiñones, los—
  mushrooms
chica—girl
chuletas—chops
cocinera—cook
comer—eat
comida—food
como—like
con—with
cuáles—which
cuándo—when
cuántos—how many
delicioso—delicious
dentro de—within

ensalada—salad
  —understand
entiendo: entender—
  understand
escoger—choose
espaguetis—spaghetti
estudiante de
  intercambio—exchange
  student
familia—family
flan, el—custard
ganar—gain
guisantes, los—peas
gustar—like
hablar—talk
hay que—one has to
hoy—today
intercambio—exchange

italiana—Italian
leche, la—milk
lechuga—lettuce
legumbres, las—vegetables
luego—then
mezcla—mixture
minutos—minutes
mirar—look
pan, el—bread
parecer—seem
peso—weight
platos—plates (of food)
poder—can, be able
poner—put
postre, el—dessert
primero—first
pudín, el—pudding

puedes: poder—can, be able
queso—cheese
refrigerador—refrigerator

sabrosa—delicious, tasty
seca—dry
sopa—soup
sopera—soup tureen
también—also

toda—all
tomar—take, have
tomate, el—tomato
zanahorias—carrots

23   Enchiladas verdes

Preguntas en adelante:

1. ¿Qué comida internacional te gusta más? ¿la italiana? ¿la china? ¿la francésa?
2. ¿Vas a un restaurante internacional a veces? ¿Qué comes?

Preguntas después de leer:

1. ¿Te gustan los chiles? ¿Te gusta la comida picante?
2. ¿Qué comida mexicana te gusta más?

Notas culturales:

1. See the additional cultural information in Answer A.
2. There are hundreds of varieties of chilies, some quite mild, and some so picante that a single brief dip in the sauce or soup is enough to make it very spicy. Just in case, wear rubber gloves when handling chilies. Some of the more common varieties are the *chile verde* or California chile (which is not the bell pepper), the *chile ancho, chile negro, chile poblano, chile serrano, chipotle, pasilla,* and *jalapeño.* Most Mexican cookbooks will describe a number of these basic chilies.
3. The Ballet Folklórico de México features carefully choreographed, colorful folk dances of Mexico. There are three performances weekly (Sunday morning and Wednesday and Sunday evenings) held in the Palacio de Bellas Artes.

Otras actividades:

1. Have students list their five favorite foreign foods. Have a student from another class tally their votes and list the top five in order. Then play *Family Feud* in class the next day.
2. Have a food day. Students may bring in Mexican food for extra credit (but no credit for tortilla chips and dip). Bring chilies and/or *picante* sauce and let students try them.
3. You might want to take a survey of local grocery stores and supermarkets to see how many and which types of chilies are available.

Suggestions for review:

Grammar review: *gustar;* stem-changing verbs *(querer, preferir; poder, probar; pedir, servir)*
Vocabulary review: taste of food; Mexican foods (see Chapter 24, Voy al *mercado*)

Vocabulary

Vocabulario para repasar en adelante:

pido: pedir—ask, order
probar—try, taste
caliente—hot
mientras—while

trabajé—I worked
guacamole—avocado salad
zócalo—plaza
quemar—burn

verduras—vegetables
frijoles—beans
sabrosas—savory, delicious
boca—mouth

Additional vocabulary—¿Cómo es la comida?

agria—sour
caliente—hot
dura—hard, tough
grasienta—greasy
picante—hot, spicy
seca—dry

amarga—bitter
deliciosa—delicious
fría—cold
nutritiva—nourishing
rico—rich

apetitosa—appetizing
dulce—sweet
insípida—bland, tasteless
jugosa—juicy
salada—salty

Pequeño diccionario:

abuela—grandmother
agua, el (f.)—water
allí—there
antes de—before
aquí—here
boca—mouth
boletos—tickets
calientes—hot
cerca (de)—close (to)
ciudad—city
comer—eat
comida—food
computadoras—computers
con—with
deber—should, ought to
diferente—different
discos—discs
dónde, donde—where
encargos—errands
esperar—wait
excelente—excellent
frijoles, los—beans

generalmente—generally
guacamole—avocado salad
hambre: tener hambre—
    be hungry
hoy—today
lentes, los—glasses
lista—list
mexicano—Mexican
mientras—while
minutos—minutes
naturales—natural (not
    crispy)
norteamericanos—
    Americans
pasado—last
pasar—stop by, pass
pido: pedir—ask, order
plato—plate
poder—can, be able
por—for
preferir—prefer

probar—try, taste
pronto—soon, fast
puedo, puedes: poder—
    can, be able
quemar—burn
restaurante—restaurant
sabrosas—tasty, savory
según—according to
servir—serve
si—if
también—also
tantas—as many
tarde—later
tienda—store
típico—typical
trabajé: trabajar—work
varios—several
verano—summer
verdes—green
verduras—vegetables
zócalo—plaza

24 Voy al mercado

Preguntas en adelante:

1. ¿Compran ustedes más comida en el mercado o en el supermercado?
2. ¿Quién en tu familia va al mercado o al supermercado?

Preguntas después de leer:

1. ¿Quién planea los menús en tu familia?
2. ¿Cuántas veces a la semana van las personas en tu familia al mercado o al supermercado?
3. ¿Dónde ves a tus amigos más a menudo? ¿Dónde los ves los fines de semana?

Notas culturales:

1. See *Encuentros culturales:* Chapter 5, *Una tortilla, por favor*; Chapter 6, *Está deliciosa;* Chapter 35, *En el mercado;* and Chapter 36, *Los americanos son ricos.*
2. *Anticuchos* are thin-sliced beef hearts, marinated and then usually grilled, although there are different recipes.
3. As more women enter the workplace, and as fewer domestic workers are available, more Hispanic families are beginning to shop once a week.
4. In nonurban areas, refrigerators are not common, in part because electricity is very expensive, so in these areas it is necessary to shop for food each day. But even those who have refrigerators shop daily in order to see their friends.

Otras actividades:

1. Have students plan supper for their family (or plan to make a casserole, or invite friends over). Then have them make a shopping list of things they'll need to buy at a market.
2. You might also want students to role-play shopping and bargaining in the market.

Suggestions for review:

Grammar review: uses of the verb *estar;* uses of *ir*
Vocabulary review: Hispanic food vocabulary (see also Chapter 21, *Pido la pizza,* and Chapter 22, *¡Cuánta comida!*); days of week

Vocabulary

Vocabulario para repasar en adelante:

carne, la—meat
puerco—pork
por supuesto—of course
pensar—think
fideos—noodles
cansada—tired

parrilla—grill
fue—did go
enseñarle—show her
ternera—veal
otra vez—again

además—besides
receta—recipe
mandar—send
sabía—I knew
ibas—you were going to

Additional vocabulary—Comida hispánica:

churros—crullers, doughnuts
paella—Spanish seafood, rice, tomato dish
frijoles refritos—similar to baked beans
tacos—tortillas with filling
chilies—chilies, peppers
flan, el—custard pudding
buñuelos—fried cookies

enchiladas—tortillas with filling cooked
tamales, los—corn dough stuffed with
  filling
aceitunas—olives
cajeta—sweet caramel-like sauce
empanadas—meat turnovers

Pequeño diccionario:

abuela—grandmother
además—besides
algo—something
americanas—American
anticuchos—Peruvian food:
  beef hearts
aquí—here
ayer—yesterday
cansada—tired
carne, la—meat
chica—girl
cocina—kitchen
comer—eat
comida—food
comprar—buy
creer—think, believe
de veras—really
decir—say
deliciosa—delicious
dormitorio—bedroom
dónde—where
enseñarle—show her
especialidad—specialty

esta noche—tonight
fideos—noodles
frutas—fruit
fue: ir—go
hamburguesas—hamburgers
hasta luego—see you later
hoy—today
ibas: ir—go
importar—be important
jueves—Thursday
legumbres, las—vegetables
luego: hasta luego—see
  you later
mandar—send
marinada—marinated
martes—Tuesday
mercado—market
miércoles—Wednesday
muchachas—girls
necesitar—need
norteamericana—American
nueva—new

otra vez—again
papas fritas—French fries
parrilla—grill
pasteles—pastries
pensar—think
peruana—Peruvian
por supuesto—of course
preparar—prepare
primera—first
probablemente—probably
puedo: poder—can, be able
puerco—pork
receta—recipe
sabía: saber—know
si—if
siento: lo siento—I'm sorry
supuesto: por supuesto—of
  course
tal: qué tal—how about
ternera—veal
toda—all
veras: de veras—really

25 La cena

Preguntas en adelante:

1. ¿Qué haces después de cenar?
2. ¿Qué comes antes de acostarte por la noche?

Preguntas después de leer:

1. ¿A qué hora cena tu familia?
2. ¿Cuándo comes más? ¿Cuándo comes demasiado?
3. ¿Cuándo comes poco? ¿Cuándo no tienes hambre?

Notas culturales:

1. See Chapter 26, *Es hora de comer*, in this volume.
2. Mealtimes depend partly on one's occupation, of course, and partly on whether one lives in a small town or city. A typical mealtime schedule for an office or store worker in a city would be as follows (give or take an hour each way): *desayuno* (breakfast) around 9:00 A.M.; *almuerzo* (lunch, equivalent to a snack or coffee break) around 12:00 noon; *comida* (main meal of the day) around 3:00 P.M.; *merienda* (snack) around 6:00 P.M.; *cena* (light supper) around 9:00 P.M.
3. Work schedules also depends on one's occupation and place of residence, of course, but a typical office worker or store employee in a city might work from 10:00 A.M. to 2:00 P.M. and 4:00 P.M. to 8:00 P.M. A typical time for young people to go the movies is around 4:00 P.M. or 6:00 P.M. More formal social events (such as parties and dances) often begin very late by American standards (11:00 P.M, for example), and last until the wee hours of the morning. Young people (but not young teens) literally dance the night away at discotheques, often arriving home at dawn.

Otras actividades:

1. You might want to take a survey to see what time supper is eaten in your community.
2. You also might want to take a survey to see how many students eat a "bedtime snack" in the evening, and what they eat. (See Chapter 21, *Pido la pizza*, for snack food vocabulary.)

Suggestions for review:

Grammar review: infinitives after impersonal expressions and prepositions *(es hora de, para, por, al, es difícil, es necesario)*
Vocabulary review: places to go in the community; time expressions versus weather expressions.

Vocabulary

Vocabulario para repasar en adelante:

acostarse—to go to bed
dijiste—you told
todavía—still

cenar—eat supper
se la presento—I'll
 introduce her (to them)

comí—I ate
aunque—although
a veces—sometimes

Additional vocabulary—Lugares adonde ir:

correo—post office
banco—bank
museo—museum
teatro—theater
tienda—store

estadio—stadium
gasolinera—gas station
parque, el—park
zoológico—zoo
centro—downtown

farmacia—drugstore
iglesia—church
supermercado—
 supermarket
cine, el—movies

Pequeño diccionario:

a qué hora—what time
a veces—sometimes
acostarse—go to bed
aeropuerto—airport
al—upon
allí—there
antes de—before
aunque—although
biblioteca—library
buen, buena—good
casa—house
cena—supper
cenar—eat supper
comer—eat
comida—meal
comí—I ate
cuando—when
de nada—you're welcome
dieta—diet
difícil—difficult
dijiste: decir—say, tell
distancia—distance
dudar—doubt
ecuatoriana—girl from
 Ecuador
entre—between
esperar—hope for
esta noche—tonight

estudiar—study
fin de semana—weekend
hacía mal tiempo—it was
 bad weather
hambre—hunger
hasta—until
helado—ice cream
hora—time
hora de—time to
importar—be important
lavar—wash
llegar—arrive
llevar—take
mal—bad
mamá—Mom
mesa—table
mirar—watch
molestarse—bother
necesario—necessary
no importa—it's not
 important
no te molestes—don't
 bother
noche, la—night
normalmente—normally
platos—dishes
por—for
por eso—that's why, for
 that reason

presentar—introduce
primero—first
problemas, los—problems
puedo: poder—can, be able
¿qué tal?—how was ...?
quitar la mesa—clear the
 table
restaurante—restaurant
Rueda de Fortuna—Wheel
 of Fortune
salir—leave
semana—week
señora—ma'am
siempre—always
también—also, too
tan—so
tanta—such a, so much
tarde—late
televisión—television
tener hambre—be hungry
tener que—have to
terminar—finish
tiempo—weather
todavía—still
tomar—take, have
viajar—travel
viaje—trip
ya—already
ya que—now that

26 Es hora de comer

Preguntas en adelante:

1. ¿Cómo es tu casa? ¿Es nueva o vieja? ¿Es bastante grande o un poco pequeña?
2. ¿Quién prepara la comida en tu casa? ¿Qué haces tú para ayudar?

Preguntas después de leer:

1. ¿Dónde come tu familia normalmente? ¿Cuándo comes en el comedor?
2. ¿Cómen ustedes las comidas congeladas? ¿Miran la televisión mientras comen?
3. ¿Tienes un patio? ¿Comen ustedes allí? ¿En qué meses?

Notas culturales:

1. See the additional cultural information in Answer B.
2. The American patio is based on the Hispanic patio (which was adapted from the Roman patio). Families in Latin America spend a lot of time, and also often eat on the patio, depending on the weather of course. The major difference is that in traditional colonial Spanish homes, the house is built around the patio, and even in modern homes, there is a wall around the patio. The Spanish patio is another room of the house, rather than a part of the yard.
3. Most houses in Latin America have separate dining and living rooms, which are usually very formal, and in many cases the activities that we do in the family room, such as watching television, playing games, sitting around, and talking to the family, are likely to be done in the master bedroom.

Otras actividades:

1. Ask students to sketch the floor plan of their house or apartment. Inside each room, have them list the activities that they do there.
2. In pairs, have students take turns describing a room. The other students guess what room it is. Or have one student name the activities that are done in a room, and the other student guess which room it is.

Suggestions for review:

Grammar review: adjective agreement
Vocabulary review: rooms of the house; outside of house (See Chapter 43, *Mi casa es tu casa);* prepositions of location (see Chapter 35, *¿Dónde está el Focolare?).*

Vocabulary

Vocabulario para repasar en adelante:

ven, vengan—come
derecha—right
afuera—outside
arriba—upstairs
ayudar—help

enseñar—show
izquierda—left
parrilla—grill
sacar—take out
listo—ready

amplia—spacious
dar a—face
ahora mismo—right now
horno—oven
olor—smell, aroma

Additional vocabulary—Los cuartos:

chimenea—fireplace,
   chimney
terreno—yard, land
dormitorio, alcoba,
   recámara—bedroom

cuarto—room
desván, el—attic
escalera—stairs
sala de recreo—rec room
entrada—entry

despensa—pantry
cuarto de baño—bathroom
sótano—basement
pasillo—hallway

Pequeño diccionario:

a comer—let's eat
acabar de—to have just
(done something)
afuera—outside
ahora mismo—right now
amplia—spacious
aquí—here
arriba—upstairs
ayudar—help
ayudarle—help you
bastante—rather, quite
bonita—pretty
buen—good
casa—house
caserola—casserole
casi—almost
cocina—kitchen
comedor—dining room
comer—eat
creer—think, believe
cuando—when
cuarto—room
dan a—face
derecha—right

dónde—where
en casa—at home
enfrente—in front, ahead
enseñar—show
grande, grandes—big
hace buen tiempo—it's
   good weather
hacer—do
hambre—hunger
hora de—time to
horno—oven
izquierda—left
lado—side
listo, lista—ready
llegar—arrive
mamá—Mom
mesa—table
minutos—minutes
moderna—modern
nada—nothing
nueva—new
olor—smell, aroma
parrilla—grill
pasar—pass, spend

poner la mesa—set the
   table
por eso—that's why, for
   that reason
por este lado—on this side
puedo: poder—can, be able
   to
puertas—doors
realidad: en realidad—in
   reality, actually
rico—rich
sacar—take out
sala—living room
sala familiar—family room
tan—so
tarde—late, later
tener hambre—be hungry
tiempo—time, weather
todo—all, everything
todos—everyone
ventanas—windows
ven: venir—come (here)
vengan: venir—come
verano—summer,
   summertime

27 ¿Vamos a comer guisantes?

Preguntas en adelante:

1. ¿Qué es una cena típica en tu casa?
2. ¿Cuánto tiempo cuesta para preparar la cena?

Preguntas después de leer:

1. ¿Qué comes en el invierno que no comes en el verano? ¿Qué comes en el verano que no comes en el invierno?
2. ¿Qué comen ustedes que está congelado?

Notas culturales:

1. See Chapter 24, *Voy al mercado,* in this volume.
2. Freezers and microwaves are almost unknown outside the major cities of Latin America, and refrigerators are found mostly in the homes of the upper middle class and well-to-do (although more urban middle-class families are beginning to acquire them). Because someone from the family goes to the market daily, and because cold drinks are believed bad for one's health, there are few refrigerators among the majority of the people. Additionally, electricity is very expensive, so electrical appliances are kept to a minimum.

Otras actividades:

1. Students might investigate the origin of the foods they eat. What foods are imported? Where are they imported from?
2. You might want students to list the electric appliances that they have in their homes (a good chance to learn this vocabulary in Spanish), and then rank them in order of their importance. If they could keep only five or six appliances, which would they keep?
3. Ask students to keep a diary for a week in which they write down all the frozen foods they eat.

Suggestions for review:

Grammar review: *gustar*-type verbs (*gustar, encantar, importar*)
Vocabulary review: food and food preparation

Vocabulary

Vocabulario para repasar en adelante:

nunca—never
dentro de—within
zanahorias—carrots
congelados—frozen

he visto—I have seen
listos—ready
sácame—take out for me

molestia—bother
guisantes, los—peas
congelador—freezer

Additional vocabulary—¿Como es la comida?

al horno—baked
cocida—cooked, boiled
frita—fried
poco asado—rare

asada—baked, roasted
cruda—raw
hervido—boiled
puré—mashed

bien cocido—well done
fresca—fresh
parrillada—grilled
término medio—medium

Pequeño diccionario:

ahora—now
aquí—here
bonita—pretty
broculi—broccoli
caer—fall
comer—eat
congelador—freezer
congelados—frozen
creer—believe
dentro—within
encantar—really like, enchant
enero—January
ensalada—salad
estudiante—student
frío—cold
guisantes, los—peas

hace frío—it's cold
hacer—do
hasta—even
he visto—have seen
hija—daughter
horno—oven
importar—be important
lechuga—lettuce
legumbres, las—vegetables
listos—ready
llegar—arrive
mesa—table
microondas, el—microwave
minutos—minutes
mirar—look
molestia—nuisance, bother
muchísimo—very, very

nieve, la—snow
nunca—never
papas al horno—baked potatoes
paquetes, los—packages
peruana—Peruvian
pongo: poner—set
preparar—prepare
pronto—soon
rosbif, el—roast beef
sacar—take out
tener hambre—be hungry
tener que—have to
todas—all
tomate, el—tomato
zanahorias—carrots

28   Es invierno, ¿sabes?

Preguntas en adelante:

1. ¿Qué tiempo hace en el invierno donde vives? ¿en el verano?
2. ¿Te sientes un poco mareado a veces cuando viajas? ¿Cómo viajas cuando te sientes así? ¿en avión? ¿en barco?

Preguntas después de leer:

1. ¿En qué aspecto geográfico depende el clima de tu región?
2. Compara el clima donde vives con el clima en Alaska y en Puerto Rico.

Notas culturales:

1. Note that this conversation, Chapter 28, and the following conversation, Chapter 29, *En San Cristóbal*, concern the same student.
2. See Chapter 44, *A las quince,* and Chapter 45, *El treinta de julio,* in this volume.
3. Chiapas is a state in southern Mexico. Tuxtla Gutiérrez, the capital of the state, is the biggest city and commercial center in the state. San Cristóbal is a regional Indian market center high in the mountains above Tuxtla Gutiérrez.
4. San Cristóbal has a substantial tourist industry today. The traditional Indian clothing, pottery, and crafts; nearby Indian villages; caves; and Mayan archaeological sites attract many visitors.

Otras actividades:

1. Do a map exercise, comparing the difference in average temperatures for Acapulco and Veracruz (*tierra caliente*) versus Mexico City and San Cristóbal (*tierra fría*). Ask students what kind of clothes they would take if they were visiting the various cities.
2. You might want to practice changing kilometers into miles and vice versa. To convert from kilometers to approximate number of miles, multiply by .6, and to convert miles to approximate number of kilometers, multiply by 1.6. (One meter is 39.36 inches.) You also might want to practice changing Celsius (centigrade) to Fahrenheit and vice versa. To convert Celsius to Fahrenheit, multiply by nine, divide by five, and add twenty-two. To convert Fahrenheit to Celsius, subtract thirty-two, multiply by five, and divide by nine.
3. Students might role-play visiting a doctor, with various complaints that a tourist might have.

Suggestions for review:

Grammar review: *gustar*-type verbs (*gustar, encantar, doler*); *sentirse.*
Vocabulary review: parts of the body; basic health expressions; weather; large numbers

Vocabulary

Vocabulario para repasar en adelante:

bienvenida—welcome	**te diviertas**—have	**sino**—but rather
subir—climb, go up	a good time	**altura**—altitude
déjame—let me	**pensar**—think	**sentirse**—feel
doler—ache	**mareados**—dizzy, nauseated	**un rato**—a while
mientras—while	**abrigo**—coat	**temporada**—period of time,
arriba—up, upstairs	**bajar**—go down	season

Additional vocabulary: El cuerpo:

boca—mouth	**brazo**—arm	**codo**—elbow	**dedos**—fingers
diente, el—tooth	**espalda**—back	**garganta**—throat	**mano, la (f.)**—hand
nariz, la—nose	**oídos**—ears	**ojos**—eyes	**pecho**—chest
pie, el—foot	**pierna**—leg	**rodilla**—knee	**tobillo**— ankle

Pequeño diccionario:

abrigo—coat	**diviertas: divertirse**—enjoy	**mejor**—better
abrir—open	yourself, have a good time	**menos de**—less than
acostumbrarse—get	**duele: doler**—ache	**metros**—meters
accustomed	**empezar**—begin	**mientras**—while
ahora—now	**encantar**—be delighted	**mil quinientos**—1500
ahorita—right now	**esta noche**—tonight	**minutos**—minutes
altura—altitude	**estómago**—stomach	**momento**—moment
aquí—here	**familia**—family	**ojalá**—I hope
arriba—up, upstairs	**festividades**—festivities	**para**—in order to
bajar—go down	**gustar**—like	**pensar**—think
bastante—rather, quite	**hacer calor**—be hot	**pies, los**—feet
bienvenida—welcome	**hacer frío**—to be cold	**poco**—little
cabeza—head	**hora**—hour	**por**—by, for
camino—road	**invierno**—winter	**prefieres: preferir**—prefer
casa—house, home	**invitarme**—invite me	**probablemente**—probably
casi—almost	**kilómetros**—kilometers	**pronto**—soon
centro—center, downtown	**llegar**—arrive	**puede: poder**—can, be able
cerca—close	**llevar**—wear	**rato**—a while
chica—girl	**mal**—ill, sick	**razón**—(be) right
curvas—curves	**mareados**—dizzy, nauseated	**regresar**—return
dentro de—within	**más de**—more than	**saber**—know
descansar—rest	**más tarde**—later	**salir**—leave
déjame—let me	**media hora**—half an hour	**semana**—week

sientes: sentirse—feel
sino—but rather
subir—climb, go up
sur, el—south
temperatura—temperature

temporada—period of time, season
turistas—tourists
ventana—window

verano—summer
viaje, el—trip
visitarles—visit you
ya—already

29 En San Cristóbal

Preguntas en adelante:

1. ¿Cuáles son las fiestas especiales que hay en la escuela?
2. ¿A qué fiesta de aquí te gustaría asistir con un visitante de otro país?

Preguntas después de leer:

1. ¿Hay días especiales que se celebran en tu región que no se celebran en otras partes? ¿Por qué son especiales?
2. ¿Hay fiestas especiales de tu iglesia o de tu nacionalidad? ¿Cómo las celebran?

Notas culturales

1. Note that the preceding conversation, Chapter 28, *Es invierno, ¿sabes?*, concerns the same students.
2. A person's saint's day or name day is celebrated much as a birthday might be celebrated here. The equivalent expression to "Happy Birthday" is *Feliz Onomástico*.
3. An interesting saint's day is celebrated in Tarija in Southern Bolivia. El Día de San Roque, the patron saint of dogs, is held in August. Dogs are decorated with ribbons and receive special blessings from the priests.
4. Indigenous populations (in Mexico, Guatemala, Peru, and Bolivia, for example) often celebrate by mixing elements of the Spanish/Christian tradition and their own native traditions. Their attire, dances, and processions, are often very colorful and interesting for Hispanic citizens and tourists alike.

Otras actividades:

1. If available, use a calendar of saints to find each student's saint's day. If they can't find their names (Keith or Ashley, for example), have them use their middle names, and if they are not listed, use the saint listed for their birth date.
2. You might want students to use the library or media center to find pictures of the traditional dress of different areas of the Spanish-speaking world. You might also ask students to come to class dressed in traditional dress, either from their own nationality, or dress that represents a part of the world. This would be a "show-and-tell" day, with each student describing his or her clothing to the class.
3. You might also want to compare the traditional images of Jesus and Mary in U.S. and Hispanic countries. For non-Catholic Americans, the role of saints in the Catholic religion might be explained to provide background for the saint's day celebrations.

Suggestions for review:

Grammar review: progressive participles
Vocabulary review: months; dates; holidays (see Chapter 48, *El desfile*).

Vocabulary

Vocabulario para repasar en adelante:

indígenas—indigenous or native peoples
misa—mass

estés: estar—be
folklóricas—folkloric, traditional

caminar—walk
carretera—road, highway

Additional vocabulary—Los meses del año:

enero—January
abril—April
julio—July
octubre—October

febrero—February
mayo—May
agosto—August
noviembre—November

marzo—March
junio—June
septiembre—September
diciembre—December

Pequeño diccionario:

abuelita—grandma
acercarse—to approach, come closer
alegrarse—be glad
allí—there
animada—animated, lively
aquí—here
así—that way
atención—attention
baile—dance
bueno—good, nice
caminar—walk
carretera—road, highway
casa—home
cintas—ribbons
claro—certainly
coche, el—car
colores—colors
con—with
dentro de—within
después—afterwards
diferente—different
divertido—fun, enjoyable
día, el—day
especial—special

esta noche—tonight
estés: estar—be
festividades—festivities
fiesta—holiday, festivity
folklóricos—folkloric, traditional
gente, la—people
gustaría: gustar—like
hablar—talk
hombres, los—men
hoy—today
iglesia—church
indígenas—indigenous people, natives
interesante—interesting
jóvenes—young people
julio—julio
llamar la atención—attract attention
llegar—arrive
mamá—mother, Mom
martes—Tuesday
minutos—minutes
mirar—look, watch
misa—Mass

mucho—a lot, much
música—music
nada más—just
noche, la—night
participar—participate
pasar—spend (time)
poco—little
por—along
¿por qué?—why?
porque—becaue
ropa—clothes, clothing
San Cristóbal de las Casas—a small city in the mountains of southern Mexico
siempre—always
sombreros—hats
tarde—later
toda—all
todos, todas—all, eveyone
vacaciones—vacation
verano—summer
veras: de veras—really
verlos—see them
visten: vestirse—dress

30 El domingo

Preguntas en adelante:

1. ¿Qué actividad especial haces los domingos?
2. ¿A qué parque vas más a menudo?
3. ¿Qué sitios de interés hay en la región donde viven ustedes?

Preguntas después de leer:

1. ¿Tienes una mesa para comer afuera de tu casa?
2. Cuando van al parque, ¿dónde comen ustedes?
3. ¿Cuándo se sientan ustedes en el suelo?
4. ¿Qué sitio en tu ciudad sería un buen lugar para hacer un picnic, estilo mexicano?

Notas culturales:

1. See additional cultural information in Answers A, B, and C.
2. The Tule tree is a two- to three-thousand-year-old giant *ahuehuete* tree about ten miles east of Oaxaca. It is more than 150 feet high and also measures about 150 feet around the base.
3. Mitla was a major religious site for the Zapotec and Mixtec Indians. The ruins at this site are elaborately inlaid with small stones in geometric patterns. There are also extensive subterranean chambers and tombs under the palaces and temples. The Hall of Columns, for example, has six giant pillars formed from single stones and is covered with a mosaic of more than 100,000 pieces of cut stone.
4. The entire city of Oaxaca is designated as a historical monument, and there is a wide agricultural ring of land around the city where no new construction is permitted. This colonial city with a strong Indian influence is also known as the Green City, because the greenish volcanic stone of which many buildings are constructed takes on a green-gold glow shortly before sunset. There are many Indian markets, both in the city and in nearby villages. In addition to Mitla, the most famous of other nearby pre-Hispanic ruins is the great city of Monte Albán, located on the summit of a hill just outside the city.

Otras actividades:

1. Have an in-class Mexican picnic. Ask students to bring in blankets. Shove desks out of the center of the room and put the blankets on the floor. Give students extra credit for bringing in Hispanic picnic foods. (You may not want to give credit for chips and dip.) Play Hispanic music. Let students practice conversing informally in Spanish.
2. You may want students to do reports on Oaxaca, Mitla, and Monte Albán.

Suggestions for review:

Grammar review: use of infinitives
Vocabulary review: picnic vocabulary

Vocabulary

Vocabulario para repasar en adelante:

camino—road
diseños—designs
mil—thousand
mantel—tablecloth
pasto—grass
frazadas—blankets

edificio—building
árbol—tree
parar—stop
sentarse—sit
florecitas—little flowers

cubierto—covered
pareció—did it seem
aire libre—outdoors,
   open air
canasta—basket

Additional vocabualry—La merienda:

abejas—bees
fuego—fire
perro caliente—hot dog
parrilla—grill
ensalada de papas—
   potato salad

banco—bench
hamburguesa—hamburger
insectos—insects
papas fritas—potato chips
sándwich—sandwich
bolsa—tote bag

frijoles refritos—beans
hormigas—ants
limonada—lemonade
mosca—fly
soleado—sunny

Pequeño diccionario:

además—besides
adónde—where
aire libre—open air
allí—there
antigüedades—antiquities,
   antiques
años—year
aquí—here
árbol, el—tree
bonito—pretty
buscar—look for
camino—road
campo—country
canasta—basket
casi—almost
cerca—close
comer—eat
cómodo—comfortable
creer—believe
cubiertos—covered
después de—after
difícil—difficult

diseños—designs
domingo—Sunday
edificios—buildings
encantar—like a lot
enfrente—ahead
esperar—wait for, expect
excursión—short trip
familia—family
florecitas—little flowers
frazadas—blankets
fue: ser—be (was)
gigantesco—giant
grande—big
gustar—like
hacer—make
hacia—towards
hambre—hunger
hasta—until
hora—time
impresionante—impressive
interesantes—interesting
izquierda—left

joven—young person
lado—side
llegar—arrive
llevar—carry
lugar, el—place
mantel, el—tablecloth
más de—more than
mesas—tables
mil—thousand
mirar—look
necesario—necessary
ningún—not any
otro—other
para—for
parar—stop
parecer—seem
parque, el—park
pasar por—pass by
pasear—drive
pasto—grass
pequeño—small
piensas: pensar—plan

planes, los—plans
poder—can, be able
por—along
¿por qué?—why?
porque—because
preciosos—precious, wonderful

restaurante—restaurant
ruinas—ruins
sentarse—sit down
sé: saber—know
sitio—site, place
sombra—shade
suerte—luck
termo—thermos

todos—all
traer—bring
ver—see
verdad—right
viejo—old
vista—view
ya—already

31 La cuenta, por favor

Preguntas en adelante:

1. ¿Qué clase de restaurante te gusta? ¿Por qué?
2. Si te casaras pronto, ¿en dónde te gustaría pasar tu luna de miel?

Preguntas después de leer:

1. En los Estados Unidos, ¿por qué traen la cuenta muy rápidamente?
2. ¿Cuáles son las diferencias entre un restaurante de servicio rápido y un restaurante elegante?

Notas culturales:

1. See the additional cultural information in Answer C.
2. The difference in the two cultures in this example is one of time. To make every minute count, Americans eat and run, one reason fast food restaurants are so popular. Hispanics, however, conduct business, build relationships, and relax while eating. Americans want the check fast, and Hispanics don't want to be rushed.
3. Cancún is a Caribbean resort on the Yucatán coast.
4. *Carne asada a la tampiqueña* is a very popular steak that is served with a tomato and chili sauce, and with Mexican specialties such as *frijoles,* guacamole, and rice.
5. Chac Mool is a reclining figure of a Mayan god. Many small stone carvings (the size of a large dog), were left throughout the Yucatán, and can be seen in many places. There is a restaurant by the same name on the beach between the Camino Real and the Krystal Hotel.

Otras actividades:

1. Field trips to Mexican restaurants or food days in class are always fun.
2. You might ask students to plan a trip to Cancún. What would they do if they had a week there? What if it were only a long weekend?
3. Have students research the Yucatán's cooking. How is it different from that of other parts of Mexico (*sopa de limas* or *cochinito pibil,* for example)?

Suggestions for review:

Grammar review: indirect object pronouns
Vocabulary review: terms of endearment; food; restaurant vocabulary

Vocabulary

Vocabulario para repasar en adelante:

luna de miel—honeymoon
miga—crumb
camarero—waiter
no me queda—it doesn't fit me

sabroso—delicious
divertirse—have a good time
bromista—kidder, joker
juntos—together

demasiado—too much
cuenta—check
traer—bring
olvidarse de—forget

Additional vocabulary—El amor

te quiero—I love you
besar—kiss
juntos—together
sentimientos—feelings
novio—boyfriend
corazón—heart
enamorado, enamorada— in love

amado, amada—beloved
amoroso, amorosa—loving
novia—girlfriend
abrazar—hug
mi vida—my darling
caricia—caress

amante—lover
te adoro—I adore you
cariñoso, cariñosa— affectionate
cariño, afecto—affection
comprometido, comprometida—engaged

Pequeño diccionario:

adónde—where
ahora—now
allí—there
aquí—here
atentos—attentive
bailar—dance
boda—wedding
bromista—kidder, joker
buen, bueno—good
camarero—waiter
camarones, los—shrimp
Cancún—Caribbean resort on the Yucatan coast
carne asada—meat, steak
Chac Mool—Cancun restaurant
comida—food
comido: comer—eat (eaten)
comí: comer—eat
con—with
cuando—when
cuenta—check
demasiado—too much
después—after
dicen: decir—say, tell

discoteca—discotheque, place to dance
divierto: divertirse—have a good time
¿dónde?—where?
especialmente—especially
estupendas—great
excelente—excellent
fantástico—fantastic
hablar—talk
hacer—do
haya—I have
he comido—I have eaten
jóvenes—young people
juntos—together
luna de miel—honeymoon
mañana—tomorrow
maravillosa—marvellous
me queda—fits me
miga—crumb
nada—nothing, not anything
ni—not even
ocupado—busy
olvidarse—forget

otro—other
pasar—spend (time), happen
pasteles, los—pastries
pastelitos—small pastries
¿por qué?—why?
por supuesto—of course
porque—but
postre, el—dessert
primero—first
probablemente—probably
puedo, puede: poder—can, be able to
queda: me queda—fits me
querer—love
querida—dear, darling
restaurante—restaurant
razón: tener razón—be right
ridículo—ridiculous
romántico—romantic
sabrosa—delicious
sirve: servir—serve
tampiqueña—Tampico style

tanto—so much

terminar—finish

todavía—still

tomar—have, eat

traiga: traer—bring

traje de baño, el—bathing
   suit

ver—see

ya—already

32 La mesa al lado de la ventana

Preguntas en adelante:

1. ¿A qué hora almuerzas en la escuela?
2. Normalmente, ¿dónde te sientas para comer? ¿Te gusta ese asiento?

Preguntas después de leer:

1. ¿A qué restaurante vas más frecuentemente? ¿Hay manteles en las mesas?
2. ¿En qué restaurantes hay manteles en la mesa?
3. ¿En qué tipo de restaurante te gusta comer cuando estás visitando otra ciudad?

Notas culturales:

Originally part of a Roman city, one of the world's largest and most impressive aqueducts is still in use in Segovia. Part of it is double-tiered. Additionally, the town is ringed by Roman walls with semicircular towers and three gates. The Alcázar was built in the 12th century, and Isabel was named Queen of Castile here in 1474. The tall cathedral is late Gothic, built in the 1500s. Magnificent views of the Guadarrama Mountains can be seen from various locations in town, including the Alcázar.

Otras actividades:

1. Have students work in pairs taking turns naming a food. The student who is listening must name the utensils that are needed to eat or drink the food.
2. You may want students to report on Ferdinand and Isabella. What else did they do besides support Columbus? Why did they support Columbus?

Suggestions for review:

Grammar review: future tense, adverbs with -*mente*
Vocabulary review: table settings; adverbs (See Chapter 42, *Nuestra casa),* prepositions of location (See Chapter 35, *¿Dónde está el Focolare?)*

Vocabulary

Vocabulario para repasar en adelante:

fortaleza—fortress	**trono**—throne	**reyes**—king and queen
tener ganas—be eager	**almorzar**—eat lunch	**quisieras**—do you want?
caminar—walk	**izquierda**—left	**adentro**—inside
bocadillos—sandwiches	**perder**—lost	**cacahuetes**—peanuts

Additional vocabulary: La mesa:

cuchara—spoon
tenedor—fork
taza—cup

cucharita—teaspoon
platillo—little plate, saucer
tazón—mug

cuchillo—knife
plato—plate, dish
vaso—glass

Pequeño diccionario:

además—besides
adentro—inside
ahora—now
algo—something
allí—there
almorzar—eat lunch
amigos—friends
antes de—before
aquí—here
así—that way
basado—based
bocadillos—snacks
buena—good
cacahuetes—peanuts
caminar—walk
casi—almost
castillo—castle
catedral, la—cathedral
católicos—Catholic
cerrado—closed
comer—eat
creer—think, believe
después de—after
esperar—wait
fortaleza—fortress

fotos—photos
ganas, las—desire
gente—people
hambre, el—hunger
hasta—until
históricos—historical
impresionante—impressive
impresionar—impress
izquierda—left
jóvenes—young people
lado: al lado de—next to
mandar—send
mesa—table
mientras—while
mirar—look
parecer—seem
pasar—pass by
perder—lose
poder—can, be able
por eso—therefore
porque—because
posiblemente—possibly
prisa: tener prisa—hurry
probablemente—probably
quisieras—do you want?

razón: tener razón—be
 right
refresco—soft drink
restaurante—restaurant
reyes—king and queen
saber—know
sacar—take (pictures)
salón, el—room
seguramente—surely
sentarse—sit, sit down
servir—serve
sitios—sites
sobre—over
solo—only
tan—so
tanto—so much
tiempo—time
tomar—have, take
traer—bring
trono—throne
varios—several
ventana—window
ver—see
veras: de veras—really?
viendo: ver—see

33 La frontera

Preguntas en adelante:

1. ¿Has visitado a otro país? ¿A cuál?
2. ¿Tienes un pasaporte?

Preguntas después de leer:

1. ¿Conoces a una persona que tiene dos nombres diferentes, que tiene un nombre o apodo en casa y otro nombre o apodo en la escuela?
2. ¿Tienes un amigo o una amiga de otro país? ¿Qué ideas diferentes tiene?
3. ¿Has estado en otro país? ¿Cómo cruzaste la frontera?

Notas culturales:

1. See Chapter 34, *Vamos a Puerto Rico*, in this volume.
2. Laredo is a major point of entry from the United States to Mexico. Thousands of tourists cross daily both to shop in Nuevo Laredo and to travel by car or bus to the interior of Mexico.
3. The customs office in Laredo is open 24 hours a day. To travel to Mexico, Americans need a Mexican tourist card, and to return, the best proof of citizenship is a United States passport. Mexican residents in Nuevo Laredo have special cards that allow them to cross easily between the two countries. However, these residents cannot travel to the interior of the United States without regular legal documents. Americans can cross into Nuevo Laredo with identification such as a driver's license, but cannot go beyond the Laredo area without a tourist card. There are checkpoints on all highways leading out of Laredo and Nuevo Laredo.
4. The Río Bravo/Rio Grande river runs from New Mexico to the Gulf of Mexico, and forms the longest border in the world marked by a single river. Other states on the border are Arizona and California.

Otras actividades:

1. Write a description of another city where many Americans cross the border in order to enter another country, either in Mexico or Canada.
2. Find out when and why the Rio Grande became the border between the two countries.
3. What can Americans take into Mexico? What can Mexicans bring to the United States? What is contraband? What *can't* legally be taken across borders?

Suggestions for review:

Grammar review: Expressions with *por*
Vocabulary review: Travel and customs vocabulary; geography (See Chapter 47, *Garrapatos*)

Vocabulary

Vocabulario en adelante:

por si acaso—just in case
cruzar la frontera—
  cross the border

mientras—while
puente, el—bridge
acercándonos—coming
  towards us

río—river
sonrían: sonreír—smile
apúrate—hurry up

Additional vocabulary—Viajes:

aduanero—customs agent
este, el—east
parada—stop, bus stop
viajero—traveller
oeste, poniente—west
sur, el—south
viaje, el—trip

boleto—ticket
excursión—short trip
gira—tour
reservas—reservations
norte, el—north
recuerdos—souvenirs
visa—visa

estación—station
jornada—journey
itinerario—itinerary
guía—guide
paseo—walk, drive
turista—tourist

Pequeño vocabulario:

acercándonos—coming
  towards us
agua, el—water
ahora—now
allí—there
amiga—friend
ancho—wide
apúrate—hurry up
aquí—here
bastante—rather, quite
bolsa—purse
buena—good
casa—house
cámara—camera
centro—center
cruzar—cross
divertido—fun
dónde—where
Estados Unidos—United
  States
estudiante—student
exacta—exact

excelente—excellent
fantástico—fantastic
foto, la—picture, photo
frontera—border
gustaría—would like
gusto—pleasure
hablar—talk
hola—hello
interesada—interested
internacional—international
invitarme—invite me
lado—side
Laredo—border city in
  Texas
línea—line
llevar—carry
marcar—mark
más tarde—later
mientras—while
mirar—look
mío—mine
necesario—necessary

Nuevo Laredo—a border
  city in Mexico
otro—another
oye—hey
papeles, los—papers
para—in order to
pasaporte, el—passport
pasar—pass
pie, el—foot
placa—placard, sign
por—for, through
por eso—therefore, that's
  why
por favor—please
¿por qué?—why?
por si acaso—just in case
prima, primo—cousin
primero—first
puente, el—bridge
quería: querer—want, wish
río—river
sacar—take

si—if

solo—only

sonrían: sonreír—smile

tarde, la—afternoon

temporada—season

todavía—yet

vámonos—let's go

visitar—visit

vista—view

vivir—live

34 Vamos a Puerto Rico

Preguntas en adelante:

1. ¿Tienes un pasaporte? ¿Adónde fuiste?
2. ¿Adónde te gusta ir de vacaciones? ¿Por qué?

Preguntas después de leer:

1. ¿A qué otro país quieres ir? ¿Qué necesitas hacer para ir allá?
2. ¿A qué otras partes del mundo puedes ir sin pasaporte?
3. ¿Qué sabes de Puerto Rico? ¿Cuál es la capital? ¿Cómo se llama el dinero allá?

Notas culturales:

1. Note the additional cultural information in Answers C and D.
2. See Chapter 33, *La frontera*, in this volume.
3. Puerto Rico is a commonwealth of the United States, but operates largely under its own constitution adopted in 1952. Most federal laws apply to Puerto Rico as if it were a state. Puerto Ricans elect their own governor and other officials. They do not pay United States income taxes, and their representative in the United States Congress is a non-voting member.
4. Puerto Rico is the only area of the United States where Columbus is believed to have landed. He claimed it for Spain, and Spain ceded the island to the United States in 1898 after the Spanish-American War. The capital of Puerto Rico is San Juan. The people are often called *borinqueños:* Borinquen was the aboriginal name of the island.

Otras actividades:

1. Ask students to find out if there are other areas of the world where passports are not necessary (i.e., Americans in Guam and the U.S. Virgin Islands, Europeans within the European Economic Community countries, etc.).
2. Ask students to find out more information about Puerto Rico. In groups of four, have students report on: 1) the geography of Puerto Rico; 2) the history of Puerto Rico; 3) the people and customs in Puerto Rico; and 4) the government of Puerto Rico.

Suggestions for review:

Grammar review: negatives
Vocabulary review: days; months (See Chapter 29, *En San Cristóbal*); seasons; names of continents

Vocabulary

Vocabulario para repasar en adelante:

adivinar—guess
país, el—country
vacunas—vaccinations
peligroso—dangerous
fuera—outside

suerte, la—luck
divertirse—enjoy oneself
sacar—get
bastante—enough
ni—neither, nor

negocios—business
envidiar—envy
ningunas—no, none,
  not any
tampoco—not either

Additional vocabulary—Los días de la semana y las estaciones del año:

lunes—Monday
jueves—Thursday
primavera—spring

martes—Tuesday
sábado—Saturday
otoño—fall, autumn

miércoles—Wednesday
domingo—Sunday
invierno—winter

Pequeño diccionario:

adivinar—guess
¿adónde?—where?
allí—there
antes—before
bastante—enough
buena, bueno—good
chicas—girls
claro—of course
con—with
conocer—meet
¿cómo es?—how is it?
cuándo—when
de todos modos—anyway
decir: es decir—that is
descansar—rest
diferente—different
divertirse—enjoy oneself,
  have a good time
días, los—days
envidiar—envy
español, el—Spanish
Europa—Europe
familia—family

fantástico—fantastic
fuera—outside
hablar—talk
has estado—have you been
hombre—man
inyecciones—injections
jóvenes—young people
llevar—take
más—more
menos—less
modos: de todos modos—
  anyway
nada—nothing, not
  anything
nadar—swim
necesario—necessary
necesitar—need
negocios—business
ni—neither, nor
ningunas—no, not any
nuevas—new
oportunidad—opportunity
país, el—country

papá—father
para—in order to
pasaporte, el—passport
peligroso—dangerous
playa—beach
practicar—practice
recuerdas: recordar—
  remember
Rusia—Russia
sacar—get, take out
salir—leave
solamente—only
suerte, la—luck
tampoco—not either
tan—so
tanta—so much
tiempo—time
toda—all
vacaciones—vacation
vacunas—vaccinations
verano—summer
¿verdad?—right?
viaje, el—trip

35   ¿Donde esta el Focolare?

Preguntas en adelante:

1. ¿Cúal es tu restaurante favorito? ¿Por qué te gusta?
2. ¿Qué haces antes de ir a un lugar nuevo?

Preguntas después de leer:

1. ¿Dónde está tu restaurante favorito? ¿Cuáles son las direcciones para ir allí de tu casa?
2. ¿Qué haces para ser cortés cuando no quieres decir la verdad?

Notas culturales:

1. See additional cultural information in Answer C.
2. The *Zona Rosa,* or Pink Zone, is one of the major tourist areas of Mexico City. There are many excellent restaurants there, as well as hotels, shops, and a market. The American embassy is just across the Paseo de la Reforma from the *Zona Rosa,* and Chapultepec Park is within walking distance.

Otras actividades:

1. Give students various locations in your community, and have them give directions to get there from school and/or from home.
2. If available (from the American Automobile Association, for example), look at a map of the *Zona Rosa* and decide what hotel Ted and Jeff may have been staying in. Also, practice giving directions to various restaurants from various hotels in the *Zona Rosa.*

Suggestions for review:

Grammar review: *ser* (identification) versus *estar* (location)
Vocabulary review: prepositions of location; vocabulary for asking and giving directions

Vocabulary

Vocabulario para repasar en adelante:

encontrarse—to meet	**doblar**—to turn	**encontrar**—to find
izquierda—left	**derecha**—right	**cuadras**— blocks
derecho derecho— straight ahead	**sigan**—continue	**próxima**—next

Additional vocabulary—Preposiciones de locación:

alrededor (de)—around
debajo (de)—under, underneath
encima (de)—on top

entre—between
delante (de)—in front
detrás (de)—in back of
enfrente (de)—facing, in front of

sobre—above, over
dentro (de)—inside
cerca (de)—near
lejos (de)—far from

Pequeño diccionario:

allí—there
aquí—here
bailes: bailar—dance
buen, buena—good
calle, la—street
Ciudad de México— Mexico City
claro—of course
comer—eat
comida—food
con—with
creer—think, believe
cuadras—blocks (city)
decir—say, tell
del—of the
derecha—right
derecho derecho—straight ahead
dice: decir—say, tell
doblar—turn
dónde—where
elegante—elegant
en—in, onto

encontrar—find
encontrarse con—to meet
esta noche—tonight
fácil—easy
grande—big
hasta—until
hermano—brother
importar—be important
izquierda, izquierdo—left
jóvenes—young people
lado—side
llamar—call
llegar—arrive
mayor—older
más tarde—later
mexicano—Mexican
música—music
nada—nothing, anything
noche, la—night
novia—girlfriend
otra vez—again
para—in order to
poco—little
policía—police officer

por—along
por favor—please
¿por qué?—why?
por supuesto—of course
programa, el—program
próxima—next
puede: poder—can, to be able to
restaurante—restaurant
saber—know
segunda—second
segura—sure
sigan: seguir—continue, follow
supuesto (see por supuesto)
tarde—late
tercera—third
típica—typical
todavía—still
un poco—a little
vayan: ir—go
ver—see
Zona Rosa—Pink Zone

36 No soy tu novia

Preguntas en adelante:

1. ¿Cuáles son las características que te gustan en la gente?
2. ¿Qué buena suerte has tenido recientemente? ¿Qué mala suerte?

Preguntas después de leer:

1. ¿Cuáles son las características que *no* te gustan en la gente?
2. ¿A qué distancia están dos personas juntas en la televisión, por ejemplo, dos comentaristas de deportes o un comentarista y un deportista (golfista, beisbolista, etc.)?

Notas culturales:

1. See also the cutural information in Answer C.
2. Ask students to notice two people standing together on television, especially on sports programs. They are probably standing shoulder-to-shoulder, much closer than the normal distance in the United States. This is approximately the distance that Hispanics normally use when interacting.
3. Hispanics (and some other nationalities as well) often perceive Americans to be unfriendly because they don't stand very close to each other when talking, and because they avoid physical contact in public, except for clearly understood exceptions (sports, dancing, etc). An American, of course, usually perceives any close physical contact as intimacy.
4. A similar Hispanic custom that Americans are unaccustomed to is that women and girls often hold hands when walking along the street together, and young men often walk side by side with their arms across each other's shoulders. These are considered signs of friendship, nothing more, and are another example of the physical closeness or contact that characterizes Hispanic relationships.
5. Another custom that often irritates American women is the *piropo*. These are complimentary remarks that Hispanic men direct toward women on the street. Hispanic women hear them but ignore them without reacting in any way, while Americans often do react physically with a disparaging look, a frown, or a faster walk. This, of course, encourages the man making the remark rather than discouraging him. *Piropos* range from the ordinary *"¡Ay, mamacita!"* to the traditional *"Tantas curvas y yo sin frenos,"* to the clever *"Tú en azul, y yo azulado (a su lado),"* for example, spoken to a woman wearing blue.

Otras actividades:

1. You might want to dramatize this conversation (and others), so that students in class get a chance to practice interacting at a closer distance. Have them pretend that it's part of a soap opera on TV.

2. In groups, have students prepare a TV script (sports interview, soap opera, two comedians, etc.), and then have them dramatize it in front of the class. Be sure the participants stand close to each other. You also may want to actually have these videotaped.

3. Ask if students in class have experiences with another culture (relatives, neighbors). They might want to relate other cultural patterns that make Americans nervous.

Suggestions for review:

Grammar review: common familiar commands, present subjunctive recognition
Vocabulary review: descriptive adjectives

Vocabulary

Vocabulario para repasar en adelante:

apúrate—hurry up	vea: ver—see	molestoso—nuisance
espérame—wait for me	suerte, la—luck	vengan: venir—come
prisa—haste	cuéntanos—tell us	ojalá—I wish
fueras—you were	intercambio—exchange	lástima—shame
párate—stop	mujer—woman	mosca—fly

Additional vocabualry—Mandatos:

acércate—come closer	aléjate—go away	bájate—get down
cállate—be quiet	diviértete—have a good time	domínate—control yourself
duérmete—go to sleep		fíjate—just imagine
levántate—stand up	pórtate bien—behave yourself	piérdete—get lost
siéntate—sit down		

Pequeño diccionario:

adónde—where	cara—face	escapar—escape
agosto—August	cerca de—close to	esperar—wait for
ahí—here	chicas—girls	Estados Unidos—United States
ahora—now	chico—boy	
alegrarse—be glad	como—like	estudiante—student
allí—there	comprar—buy	feliz—happy
amable—kind	con—with	Filadelfia—Philadelphia
apurarse—hurry	creer—think, believe	fueras: ser—be
bastante—rather, quite	cuándo—when	guapo—cute
buenas—good	cuéntanos—tell us	hablar—talk
calmarse—calm down	digo: decir—tell	hasta luego—see you later

insistente—insistent
intercambio—exchange
lástima—shame
mala—bad
más tarde—later
mientras—while
mira—look
molestoso—annoying
mosca—fly
mujer—woman
noticias, las—news
novia—girlfriend
nuevo—new
ojalá—I hope, I wish

oye—hey
padre—terrific
pararse—stop
pasar—happen
poco—little
poder—can, be able to
¿por qué?—why?
prisa—haste
pronto—soon
próximo—next
puedas, puedo: poder—
  can, be able to
refresco—soft drink
saber—know
salir—leave

siempre—always
simpático—nice
suerte, la—luck
también—also
tan—so
tarde—late
tipo—type
traigo: traer—bring
vea: ver—see
vengan: venir—come
verdad—right
vernos—see each other
vez—time
viene: venir—come

37 Besos olvidados

Preguntas en adelante:

1. ¿Miras las telenovelas, o *soap operas,* de los Estados Unidos? ¿Cuáles miras?
2. ¿Qué prefieres, ver la televisión o ir al cine?

Preguntas después de leer:

1. ¿Cuál de los últimos episodios de programas famosos has visto? ¿Por qué fue notable?
2. ¿Te gustan las *mini-series*? ¿Miras todas las noches?
3. ¿Cuánto tiempo debe durar una *mini-serie*? ¿dos noches? ¿cinco noches? ¿más?
4. ¿Crees que serían populares las telenovelas en los Estados Unidos? ¿Te gusta la idea de un cuento que dura dos o tres meses? ¿Por qué?

Notas culturales:

1. Note that this *telenovela* is fictitious, as are the three stars' names listed.
2. Note the additional cultural information in Answer B and Answer D.
3. *Telenovelas* from Venezuela are currently charming Spanish audiences; they love the accent. *Cristal* was the first big Venezuelan hit.
4. María Conchita Alonso, now fairly well known here in the United States, started as an actress on a *telenovela.* Many top stars are willing to star in a *telenovela* because it is not a long-term commitment.
5. Notice the time at which the main meal of the day is eaten and what time the telenovela is on.

Otras actividades:

1. If available, you might want students to read an article about a *telenovela* or a telenovela star in a magazine like *Más,* a magazine for Hispanics in the United States, or in such Hispanic magazines as *Tú, Coqueta,* or *Hola.*.
2. Look at a television listing from a Hispanic newspaper. Try to guess which programs might be *telenovelas.* What time are they on?

Suggestions for review:

Grammar review: present perfect
Vocabulary review: television vocabulary

Vocabulary

Vocabulario para repasar en adelante:

telenovela—similar to soap opera
muriera—died
se resuelva—it's resolved
al revés—the opposite
hasta—even

besos—kisses
me encuentro con—I'll meet
papel, el—part, role
dejar plantado—jilt, break up with

olvidados—forgotten
cuento—story
de acuerdo—I agree
carrera—career
pegada a la pantalla—glued to the screen

Additional vocabualry—La televisión y el cine:

programa concurso—game show
cable—cable
televidentes—TV viewers
comedia—drama
pronóstico del tiempo—weather forecast
filmar—to film
programa policíaco—police show
red, la—network
anuncio comercial—commercial
grabar—to record

documental, el—documentary
canal, el—channel
programa cómico—comedy
película—movie
locutor, locutora—announcer
noticias, las—news
televisor, el—TV set
estrella—star
cómico—comedian
horario—schedule

Pequeño diccionario:

actriz—actress
acuerdo: de acuerdo—agreed
amigas—friends
año—year
besos—kisses
cancelar—cancel
carrera—career
chica—girl
cine, el—movies
¡claro que sí!—Of course!
comer—eat
creer—think, believe
cuento—story
dejó: dejar plantado—jilt, break up with
después de—after
distinguido—distinguished
día, el—day
durante—during
encuentro: encontrarse con—meet

episodio—episode
estado: estar—be
fantástica- fantastic, great
favorita—favorite
guapo—cute
hablar—talk
hasta—even
hombre—man
hoy—today
importar—be important
lástima—shame
mañana—tomorrow
maravillosa—wonderful, marvelous
mejor—better
mejorar—improve
mexicanas—Mexican
moderno—modern
mujer—woman
muriera—died
normalmente—normally
ocurrir—occur

ojalá—I hope
olvidados—forgotten
otra—another
pantalla—screen
papel, el—part
pegada—glued
plantado: dejar plantado—jilt, break up with
populares—popular
probablemente—probably
programa—program
razón: tener razón—be right
repetir—repeat
resuelva: resolver—resolve
revés—reverse
saber—know
salir—leave
semanas—weeks
sido: ser—be

siempre—always

tan—so

tarde—afternoon, late

telenovela—soap opera

temprano—early

terminar—end, finish

todo—everything

última—last

ver—see

vez: de vez en cuando—from time to time

vi, visto: ver—see

ya—already

como—as

con—with

cuál—which one

más—most

para—in order to

¿por qué?—why?

porque—because

también—also

verdad—true

38 Las rosas, sí

Preguntas en adelante:

1. ¿Qué puede hacer un joven a quien le gusta una chica? ¿Qué puede mandarle? Hoy día, ¿mandan flores las chicas a los muchachos?
2. ¿Tiene tu estado una flor oficial? ¿Cuál es?

Preguntas después de leer:

1. ¿Hay flores en los Estados Unidos que son para una sola ocasión específica, nada más?
2. ¿Cuáles son tus flores favoritas? ¿Te gustaría recibir un ramo o una planta de estas flores?

Notas culturales:

1. Note that the following conversation, Chapter 39, *Es un buen precio,* concerns the same students.
2. For more information on death, see Chapter 50, *¡Uy, qué horrible!* in this volume.
3. Flowers are actually very inexpensive. Roses are sold in enormous bunches of two to three dozen for a couple of dollars along the road outside Cuernavaca, Mexico, for example. For this reason, many hotels put fresh flowers in rooms, and many Mexican homes are decorated with bouquets of fresh flowers.
4. While not as widespread as in the past, there is still a language of flowers. As here in the United States, certain flowers are associated with certain holidays. *Caléndulas,* for example, are associated with the *Día de los Muertos,* on November 2. And certain flowers are associated with various saints. In México, one always takes roses to the Shrine of Guadalupe, because according to legend, roses bloomed in the desert where she appeared.
5. Flower vocabulary: *diente de león* (dandelion); *caléndula* (marigold); *geranio* (geranium); *girasol* (sunflower); *lirio del valle* (lily of the valley); *hortensia* (hydrangea); *jacinta* (hyacinth); *pensamiento* (pansy); *orquídea* (orchid; *nomeolvides* (forget-me-not); *ranúnculo* (buttercup).

Otras actividades:

1. Review the seasons by asking students to list the flowers that are typical of each season. Review holidays by asking students to name flowers that are popular for each holiday.
2. You might want to have students make Mexican-style paper flowers in class.

Suggestions for review:

Grammar review: comparatives; past tense of *ir* and *divertirse* (Even if students have not yet studied the past tense, you might want to introduce these two useful verbs and practice them as vocabulary rather than grammar.)
Vocabulary review: stores, descriptive adjectives, flowers

Vocabulary

Vocabulario para repasar en adelante:

conoció—met
cuestan: costar—cost
margaritas—daisies
apropiada—appropriate
crisantemas—
chrysanthemums

anoche—last night
darse cuenta—realize
fíjate—notice
claveles, los—carnations
demasiado—too

mandarle—send her
puestos—stands, stalls
azucenas—lillies
cesta—basket
ramo—bouquet

Additional vocabulary—Las tiendas:

carnicería—meat market
galletería—cookie shop
juguetería—toy store
panadería—bakery
librería—bookstore
tarjetería—card shop

dulcería—candy shop
heladería—ice cream store
lechería—dairy store
pastelería—pastry shop
pescadería—fish market
zapatería—shoe store

frutería—fruit stand
joyería—jewelry store
perfumería—perfumes,
makeup
taquería—taco stand

Pequeño diccionario:

anoche—last night
apropiadas—appropriate
aquí—here
azucenas—lilies
Bogotá—capital of
Colombia
bonita—pretty
cantidad—quantity
cestas—baskets
chica—girl
claveles, los—carnations
comprar—buy
con—with
concierto—concert
conmigo—with me
conoció: conocer—meet
creer—think, believe
créme—believe me
crisantemos—
chrysanthemums

cuenta: darse cuenta—
realize
cuestan: costar—cost
demasiado—too
divertí: divertirse—have a
good time, enjoy oneself
doy: darse cuenta—realize
e—and
enorme—enormous
Estados Unidos—United
States
estuvo: estar—be (was)
fabuloso—fabulous
feria—fair
fin de semana—weekend
fíjate—notice (something)
florería—flower shop
flores, las—flowers
grande—big
hacer—do

inteligente—intelligent
joven—young person
mandar—send
mandarle—send her
margaritas—daisies
mejores—better
mercado—market
mirar—look, look at
muchacha—girl
norteamericano—American
otra vez—again
pequeño—small
prima—cousin
pueden: poder—can, be
able to
puestos—stands, stalls
ramo—bouquet, flower
arrangement
rosas—roses
saber—know

salir—go out

semana—week

simpática—nice

tal: qué tal—what about

verdad—right

vez: otra vez—again

39   Es un buen precio

Preguntas en adelante:

1. ¿Cuáles son los factores que usas para decidir en dónde comprar una cosa?
2. ¿Compras flores? ¿Para qué ocasión?

Preguntas después de leer:

1. ¿Qué cosa compramos para que podamos negociar el precio en los Estados Unidos?
2. ¿En qué circunstancias es posible recibir un descuento aquí?
3. ¿Cómo sabemos que lo que pagamos es el mejor precio?

Notas culturales:

1. Note that the previous conversation, Chapter 38, *Las rosas, sí,* concerns the same students.
2. Notice the additional cultural information in Answer A and Answer D.
3. There is a word in Spanish for helping friends: *amiguismo.* One facet is the practice of giving discounts in stores that they manage or own. The closer the friend, the greater the discount. Almost anyone can get 10 percent off, friends may get 20 percent off, close friends 30 to 40 percent off, and family and *compadres* get a price that is the wholesale price or a fraction above it, depending, of course, on the markup of the item.
4. Having friends makes life easier in Mexico. If one has to pay a fine, for example, having a friend who knows someone in court will reduce or eliminate the fine. If one needs a permit, a license, or official approval, for example, having a friend will help one acquire them faster and with less bureaucratic involvement. Friends help with weddings (see Chapter 41, *Las madrinas,* in this volume, for example), with baptisms, with anniversaries, with funerals, and all types of events.

Otras actividades:

1. First have students make a list of things they do for their friends; then have them make a list of things their friends do for them. After that, have them categorize their friends as *compadre/comadre, amigo/amiga,* or *conocido/conocida.*
2. Have students practice bargaining. In advance, have students collect pictures of merchandise they might sell in the market (clothes, food, shoes and leather goods, pottery, flowers, etc.). You might want to set up a mock market with about half of the students playing the role of salesperson, and half playing the role of customer.

Suggestions for review:

Grammar review: demonstrative adjectives and pronouns; *más que* versus *más de*
Vocabulary review: shopping vocabulary

Vocabulary

Vocabulario para repasar en adelante:

mandar—send	**conocidos**—acquaintances	**en vez de**—instead of
caminar—walk	**ramos**—bouquets,	**deber**—ought to, should
docena—dozen	arrangements	**dije**—I told
florería—flower shop	**muestra**—display	**precio**—price
or stand	**vimos**—we saw	**compadre**—relationship
		between godfather and
		father; very close friend

Additional vocabulary—De compras:

barato—cheap, inexpensive	**cliente**—client, customer
descuento—discount	**bolsa**—bag
caja—cash register, place to pay	**caro**—expensive, pricey
cheque—check	**ganga**—bargain
etiqueta—price tag	**en efectivo**—in cash
mostrador—counter	**paquete, el**—package
surtido—assortment, stock	**tarjeta de crédito**—credit card
selección—selection	**recibo**—receipt
¿En qué puedo servirle?—May I help you?	**vendedor**—salesperson
venta—sale	**¿Qué precio tiene?**—What's the price?
¿Cuánto cuesta?—How much does it cost?	

Pequeño diccionario:

además—besides	**compadre**—close friend	**florería**—flower shop
allí—there	**comprar**—buy	**flores, las**—flowers
antes (de)—before	**conocidos**—acquaintances	**importar**—be important
aquel—that	**conozco: conocer**—know	**joven**—young person
aquí—here	**costar**—cost	**malos**—bad
autobús, el—bus	**dar**—give	**mandar**—send
bastante—enough	**deber**—ought to, should	**más de**—more than
básico—basic	**dices, digo: decir**—say	**mejor**—best
buen, bueno—good	**dije: decir**—say, tell	**mercado**—market
buscar—look for	**dinero**—money	**mirar**—look, look at
calidad—quality	**docena**—dozen	**mismo: aquí mismo**—right
caminar—walk	**dónde**—where	here
cantidad—quantity	**dueños**—owners	**muchísimas**—a great many
casa—house, home	**enfrente**—ahead	**muestra**—display
chica—girl	**enorme**—enormous	**mujeres**—women
como—as	**espectaculares**—spectacular	**nada más**—that's all

otras—other
oye—hey
para—for, to
por eso—that's why
¿por qué?—why?
porque—because
precio—price
preciosos—lovely
probablemente—probably

propietario—proprietor, manager
puedo: poder—can, be able
puesto—stand
ramos—bouquets, flower arrangements
recibir—recieve
rinconcito—small corner
rosa—rose

segundo—second
sola—single
tan—so
tío—uncle
todas—all
vender—sell
ver—see
vez: en vez de—instead of
vimos: ver—see

40 Las bodas de Angélica

Preguntas en adelante:

1. ¿Te gusta ir a las bodas?
2. ¿Por qué cuestan mucho dinero las bodas?

Preguntas después de leer:

1. ¿Tienes una madrina? ¿Cuántos años tiene?
2 ¿Has participado en unas bodas? ¿Cómo? ¿Qué hiciste?

Notas culturales:

1. Note that the following conversation, Chapter 41, *Las madrinas,* concerns the same students.

2. See the additional cultural information in Answer B and Answer D.

3. Note that in some countries, bridesmaids are *damas de honor*, and the matron of honor is the *madrina de bodas*.

4. Since a government may not recognize a church wedding, and vice versa, in many Hispanic countries couples have multiple wedding ceremonies: one for the church performed by a priest, minister, or other member of the clergy, and one civil ceremony performed by a judge. Sometimes indigenous couples have a third ceremony, the traditional native ceremony. In this country, of course, we must get the government's permission (wedding license) in order to get married, no matter where or how we do it.

5. You might want to mention *Bodas de sangre (Blood Wedding)* by Federico García Lorca, which is probably the best known of all plays in Spanish. Other expressions like *bodas de plata* (silver anniversary); *bodas de oro* (golden anniversary); and *bodas de diamante* (diamond anniversary), are used for anniversaries other than weddings, and are also used in the sense of, for example, a silver jubilee.

6. Many of our wedding traditions are not observed in Mexico. The bride dresses at home and is driven to the church. After arriving at the church and before the wedding, the bride may let the groom know she's arrived, and may chat with him and with many of the late-arriving wedding guests before the ceremony.

Otras actividades:

Try to find a copy of the text for a wedding ceremony in Spanish (many churches have Spanish versions, for example). Then hold a mock wedding in class. (See the suggestion in *Las madrinas,* Chapter 41, first.)

Suggestions for review

Grammar review; age, possessive adjectives; the words *e* and *u*.
Vocabulary review: wedding vocabulary; relatives

Vocabulary

Vocabulario en adelante:

bodas, las—wedding
novia—bride

madrina—godmother, benefactor
divertirse—enjoy oneself

Additional vocabulary—Las bodas:

altar—altar
casarse—get married
cura, sacerdote, el—priest
invitado—guest
matrimonio—married couple
pastel de bodas, el—wedding cake
testigos—witnesses

anillo de boda—wedding ring
dedo anular—ring finger
juez—judge
novio—groom
pastor—minister, pastor
ramillete, el—corsage
velo—veil

banco—church pew
ceremonia—ceremony
iglesia—church
luna de miel—honeymoon
pasadizo—aisle
rabino—rabbi
ramo de flores—bouquet
recién casado—recently married, newlywed

Pequeño diccionario:

amigas—friends
aquí—here
bodas—wedding
bonitas—pretty
buenas—good
como—as
conocer—to know
¿cuántas?—how many?
dama de honor—maid of honor
decir—to say, tell
e—and
fiesta—party
fin de semana—weekend

hacer—to do, to make
hermana—sister
hija—daughter
jóvenes—young, young people
madrina—godmother, bridesmaid
madrina de bodas—bridesmaid
mamá—mother
mayor—older
novias—brides
otra, otras—other, another
por eso—therefore
porque—because

prima—cousin
probablemente—probably
que—than
razón: tener razón—be right
saber—to know
sábado—Saturday
seguro—sure
semana—week
sé (see saber)
tan—as
u—or
verdad—right
ya—already

41 Las madrinas

Preguntas en adelante:

1. ¿Qué es necesario planear antes del día de las bodas?
2. Si te casaras muy pronto, ¿a qué amigos o amigas invitarías a participar en las bodas?

Preguntas después de leer:

1. ¿Has participado en unas bodas? ¿Qué tienes que hacer para prepararte?
2. ¿Sabes cuánto cuesta aquí para hacer unas bodas tradicionales?
3. ¿Quién paga o ayuda a pagar?
4. ¿Cuáles son las ventajas y las desventajas de las bodas al estilo mexicano?

Notas culturales:

1. Note that the preceding conversation, Chapter 40, *Las bodas de Angélica,* concerns the same students.
2. See Chapter 38, *Las rosas, sí,* in this volume.
3. One definition of *madrina* is bridesmaid, and in Mexico *madrinas* also usually fit this definition, but in other countries the *madrinas* and *padrinos* are sponsors. While they are attendants and may stand at the altar with the bridal couple, they are not typical bridesmaids and best men.
4. Santa Prisca, which faces the *zócalo,* is the largest church in Taxco. It was built in the mid-18th century and paid for by one man, José de la Borda, who made a fortune in the Taxco silver mines. The reason he gave for his generosity was, "What God gives to Borda, Borda gives to God." The church is probably Mexico's finest example of baroque architecture.
5. Locate Cuernavaca on a map of Mexico. It is south of Mexico City. Then locate Taxco (south of Cuernavaca) and Iguala (south of Taxco). Many wealthy families from Mexico City have second homes in Cuernavaca, the city of flowers. Cortés' summer palace is there. Taxco, the silver capital, is built high on a mountainside. Its colonial style has been preserved.

Otras actividades:

1. You might want to have students choose two television characters and pretend that they are going to marry each other. Then have them describe the wedding. Or have them invent an imaginary Mexican that they will marry, and describe the wedding: where, when, what church, who will be in it, flowers, etc.

2. If you have decided to have a mock wedding (see *Las bodas de Angélica,* Chapter 40), have students pick out *madrinas* or *padrinos* in the Mexican fashion and list them in the program for the wedding.

Suggestions for review:

Grammar review: *acabar de* and *ir a.*
Vocabulary review: Equivalents for "good," "wonderful," etc.; wedding vocabulary (See Chapter 40, *Las bodas de Angélica*), terms of endearment (See Chapter 31, *La cuenta, por favor*)

Vocabulary

Vocabulario para repasar en adelante:

bodas, las—wedding	**acabar de**—just	**ramo**—bouquet
florería—florist shop	**madrina**—bridesmaid	**velo**—veil
traer—bring	**inesperado**—unexpected	**tejiendo: tejer**—weave
corona—crown	**chiste, el**—joke	**aliviada**—relieved

Additional vocabulary—Buenos adjectivos:

admirable—admirable, wonderful	**afortunado**—fortunate, lucky
atractiva—attractive	**bien parecido**—good-looking, handsome
dichosa—happy, lucky	**elegante**—elegant
estupendo—stupendous, wonderful	**fantástico**—fantastic, great
bello—beautiful	**formidable**—formidable, wonderful
guapa—cute, good-looking	**increíble**—incredible
interesante—interesting	**maravillosa**—marvelous
suerte: tener suerte—be lucky	**fabuloso**—fabulous
tremendo—tremendous	**perfecto**—perfect

Pequeño diccionario:

acabar de—have just (done something)	**conozco: conocer**—know	**hacer**—do
ahora—now	**corona**—crown	**haya: hay**—there is, there are
aliviada—relieved	**Cuernavaca**—Mexican city	**hermana**—sister
allí—there	**decirme**—tell me	**hermano**—brother
amigas—friends	**dice, dicen: decir**—say, tell	**hermosísimas**—very beautiful
aquí—here	**dónde**—where	**hola**—hi
blancas—white	**entiendo: entender**—understand	**idea**—idea
bodas, las—wedding	**esperar**—hope	**iglesia**—church
bonitas—pretty	**esta tarde**—this afternoon	**Iguala**—Mexican city
buena—good	**familia**—family	**inesperado**—unexpected
chiste, el—joke	**florecitas**—small flowers	**lindas**—pretty
con—with	**florería**—florist shop	**listo**—ready
conocer—know, meet	**flores, las**—flowers	

llamar—call
llevar—take
madrina—bridesmaid
magnífico—great,
  wonderful
malo—bad
margaritas—daisies
más tarde—later
médico—doctor
mirar—look
muuuuy: muy—very
nada—nothing, not
  anything

oye—hey
papá—father
para—for, in order to
pastel, el—cake
pastel de bodas, el—
  wedding cake
por—through, for the
  purpose of
¿por qué?—why?
preciosas—precious,
  wonderful
primero—first
quién—who

ramos—bouquets
rosas—roses
segura—sure
tantos—so man
tejiendo: tejer—weave
todavía—still
traerlas—bring them
velo—veil
ver—see
vestido—dress
ya verás—you'll see
zócalo—plaza

42 Nuestra casa

Preguntas en adelante:

1. ¿A quiénes se invitan mucho a tu casa? ¿A quiénes se invitan en general?
2. ¿Dónde está tu casa en relación al centro de la ciudad grande más cercana? ¿Está a 20 minutos o a dos horas, por ejemplo?
3. ¿Dónde está tu casa en relación al aeropuerto?

Preguntas después de leer:

1. ¿Cómo es el barrio donde vives?
2. ¿Hay turistas o extranjeros que visitan tu barrio? ¿Cuál es el sitio más cercano que quieren visitar los turistas?

Notas culturales:

1. See Chapter 43, *Mi casa es tu casa*, in this volume.
2. San Isidro is the most elegant residential district of Lima. Just beyond is Miraflores, an elegant city and beautiful resort town that sits on a cliff overlooking the Pacific. The main streets are well lit and there are shops, restaurants, parks, street vendors, sidewalk cafés, and theaters. Another nice area is Pueblo Libre, where there are many examples of colonial architecture.
3. Costa Verde is a string of beaches nearby, but while strolling and eating there are popular, swimming is not. The water is cold and polluted, there is a strong undertow, and jellyfish are common. The safe and relatively clean beach areas begin 25 to 30 miles south of Lima.

Otras actividades:

1. You might want to discuss other English words borrowed from Spanish ("patio," for example). Is the connotation the same in both languages?
2. You might want students to prepare a tourist booklet about their own town, suburb, or part of the city.

Suggestions for review:

Grammar review: direct object pronouns; pronouns attached to the infinitive (*verte, encontrarnos, encontrarme, invitarnos, conocerlos, enseñarnos); por* and *para*
Vocabulary review: adverbs; idiomatic expressions (*acabar de..., gracias por..., con anticipación, tener ganas de..., estar a..., darse cuenta de que..., vámonos,* etc.)

Vocabulary

Vocabulario para repasar en adelante:

regresar—return
con anticipación—looking
   forward to

venir—come
tener ganas—be eager
barrio—area, district

di cuenta—realized
listo—ready
venga—come

Additional vocabulary—Adverbios:

afortunadamente—fortunately
constantemente—constantly
evidentemente—evidently
generalmente—generally
normalmente—normally
probablemente—probably
recientemente—recently
típicamente—typically

claramente—clearly
diariamente—daily
exactamente—exactly
inmediatamente—immediately
obviamente—obviously
rápidamente—rapidly
seguramente—surely

Pequeño diccionario:

acabar de—have just (done
  something)
alegrarse—be happy
anticipación—anticipation,
  looking forward to
aquí—here
Arequipa—city in Peru
avenida—avenue
barrio—district, area, barrio
bueno—good
casa—house
centro—downtown, center
ciudad—city
comer—eat
con—with
conocerlos—meet (you)
cuenta (see di cuenta)
de veras—really
di cuenta—realize
encantar—delight, enchant
encontrarnos—meet us
enseñarnos—show us
entre—between
esperar—expect
esta noche—tonight
estudiante—student
familia—family

francamente—frankly
ganas: tiene ganas—is
  eager
gracias por—thanks for
hablar—talk
hola—hi
iglesias—churches
igualmente—same, equally
invitarnos—invite us
lejos—far
Lima—capital city of Perú
listos—ready
llamarse—be called, named
mamá—mom
mañana—tomorrow
minutos—minutes
Miraflores—a suburb of
  Lima
molestarse—be bothered
museos—museums
nada más—nothing more,
  that's all
naturalmente—naturally
norteamericana—American
nuestra—our
otra vez—again
padres—parents

papá—Dad
para—for, in order to
parte—part
peruana—Peruvian
poder—can, be able to
por—for, along
por fin—finally
posible—possible
posiblemente—possibly
preparar—prepare
puede: poder—can, be able
  to
regresar—return
restaurante—restaurant
San Isidro—a suburb of
  Lima
seguro—sure
todo, todos—all, everything
vámonos—let's go
venga: venir—come
veras: de veras—really
verte, verles—see you
viajar—travel
vienen: venir—come
visita—visit
vivir—live

43 Mi casa es tu casa

Preguntas en adelante:

1. ¿Cómo es tu casa?
2. ¿Cuáles son los peligros donde vives?

Preguntas después de leer:

1. ¿Hay una muralla o una cerca fuera de tu casa? ¿Está enfrente o detrás de la casa?
2. ¿Hay un lugar de retiro fuera de tu casa?

Notas culturales:

1. Note the additional cultural information in Answer B.
2. You might want to discuss the concept of privacy in the two cultures. We guard our privacy only inside our homes, while Hispanics want privacy both inside and outside their homes.
3. Some houses, of course, are built in colonial Hispanic style. They are built around a central patio and the front walls border the sidewalks. There are bars or strong shutters on the windows and a gate or heavy doors at the front entrance. The houses fill the lots, and if the lot is small and the house is an "L" shape, for example, there are walls at the side and back surrounding the patio.
4. In most Hispanic cities there is no zoning, so that very poor houses (with no lawns and with animals such as chickens or a goat) may be built adjacent to very impressive houses. In such cases, the walls of the more expensive homes may enclose a nice lawn and a pretty well-cared-for garden and flowers, and shut out what might otherwise be a disturbing view.

Otras actividades:

1. If pictures are available, you may want to compare and contrast traditional houses in your area of the country with traditional Spanish-style houses.
2. Have students bring snapshots of their own house or a magazine picture of a dream house. Then have them describe the house to a partner.

Suggestions for review:

Grammar review: possessive adjectives and possessive pronouns; *hace* + time
Vocabulary review: vocabulary to describe outside of house; rooms of house (see Chapter 26, *Es hora de comer*).

Vocabulary

Vocabulario para repasar en adelante:

izquierda—left
bajar—get off of
peligro—danger
ladrones—robbers, thieves
terreno—land, yard, field

claxón, el—horn
muralla—wall
terremotos—earthquakes
barrio—neighborhood
vecinos—neighbors

portal, el—gate
alrededor—around
asesinos—assassins
nos conviene—suits us

Additional vocabulary: Fuera de la casa

acera, anden, banqueta—
  sidewalk
calle, la—street
chimenea—chimney,
  fireplace
jardín, el—garden
pararrayos, el—lightning rod
patio—patio
vecindad—vicinity

azotea—sun roof, flat roof
balcón, el—balcony
cerca—fence
contraventanas—shutters
garaje, el—garage
pajarera—birdhouse
parrilla—grill
plantas—plants
techo—roof

árboles, los—trees
barandilla—railing
césped, el—lawn
flores, las—flowers
granero—barn
matas—bushes
pasto—grass
pórtico, porche—porch

Pequeño diccionario:

a casa—home
a veces—at times
abrir—open
abuelos—grandparents
acaba de—just (did
  something)
adonde—where
ahora—now
allí—there
alrededor—around
años—years
aquí—here
arriba—upstairs
asesinos—assassins
aunque—although
bajar—get out
barrio—neighborhood
bienvenido—welcome
bonita—pretty
bueno—well
calle, la—street
carro—car
casa—house
casi—almost
ciudad—city

claxón, el—horn
comer—eat
conviene: convenir—suit,
  agree with
cómoda—comfortable
crimen, el—crime
cuarto—room
¿cuánto tiempo hace?—
  how long?
después—afterwards
detrás—behind
digo: decir—say, tell
Dios—God
dormitorio—bedroom
familia—family
fácil—easy
fin, el—end
gato—cat
hermanas—sisters
hora—hour
inmediatamente—
  immediately
izquierda—left
jardín, el—garden
lado—side

ladrones—robbers, thieves
llegar—arrive
más de—more than
miedo—fear
momento—moment
muralla—wall
nada—nothing
norteamericano—American
otro—other
padres—parents
para—in order to
pasado—past
peligro—danger
pequeño—small
permitir—permit, let
permíteme—let me
perro—dog
poder—can, be able to
por fin—finally
¿por qué?—why?
portal, el—gate
preocuparse—to be worried
puerta—door
quieramos: querer—want
salir—leave, go out

siempre—always

tener miedo—be afraid

terremotos—earthquakes

terreno—land, yard, field

tiempo—time

tocar—to honk

todos—all

tranquilo—quiet

veces—times

vecinos—neighbors

veinte—twenty

ver—see

viene: venir—come

vivir—live

44 A las quince

Preguntas en adelante:

1. ¿Adónde va tu familia de vacaciones? ¿Prefieren ustedes ir al campo, las grandes ciudades o a la playa?

2. ¿Visitan ustedes a amigos o parientes cuando van de vacaciones? ¿quiénes?

3. ¿Cuándo sale tu familia de vacaciones?

Preguntas después de leer:

1. ¿Quiénes usan el reloj de 24 horas en este país?

2. ¿A qué hora terminan las clases en tu escuela según el reloj de 24 horas? ¿A qué hora cenan ustedes? ¿A qué hora te acuestas (vas a la cama)?

Notas culturales

Viña del Mar is a fashionable seacoast resort on the Pacific coast just to the northwest of Santiago. Its excellent climate and wide beaches make it one of the most popular resorts in South America.

Otras actividades:

1. Ask students to use the 24-hour clock to prepare their schedule of classes.

2. You might also want students to use the 24-hour clock to prepare a list of their favorite television programs or to prepare one night's television schedule. Additionally, you can ask students to work in pairs. One student gives the day, time, and channel for a television show, and the other student tries to guess the name of the show.

3. Ask students to pretend that a Chilean friend is going to spend a weekend with them. Have them prepare a schedule of activities that will help the visitor get to know your town or city and give him or her a sample of typical weekend activities for American young people.

Suggestions for review:

Grammar review: dates; time; weather; forms of *ir, poder*
Vocabulary review: transportation; family members (See Chapter 9, *Sí, señorita*); days of week (See Chapter 34, *Vamos a Puerto Rico*)

Vocabulary

Vocabulario para repasar en adelante:

divertirnos—to enjoy
  ourselves
lugar, el—place
suerte, la—luck

esperar—to wait, to expect
poder—to be able
buscar—to look for

último—last
horario—schedule   lugar,
sorprenderse—to be
  surprised

Additional vocabulary—El transporte:

a caballo—on horseback
automóvil, el—automobile
bicicleta—bicycle
crucero—cruise ship
metro—subway
tren, el—train
submarino—submarine
velero—sailboat

a pie—on foot
camioneta—van,
  station wagon
diligencia—stagecoach
funicular, el—inclined railway
vapor, el—steamship
motocicleta—motorcycle

autobús, camión—bus
barco—boat
carro, coche—car
lancha—motorboat
helicóptero—helicopter
teleférico, gondolas—cable
cars

Pequeño diccionario:

¿a qué hora?—What time?
a veces—sometimes
allí—there
antes—before
anticipación—anticipation
año—year
aquí—here
así—thus
aunque—although
autobús, el—bus
bastante—rather, quite
bueno, buena—good
buscar—look for
carro—car
clase, la—class
con—with
creer—think, believe
desierto—desert
después—after
diciembre—December
divertirse—enjoy oneself
día, el—day
durante—during
en punto—sharp

en vez de—instead of
escritorio—desk
especialmente—especially
esperar—expect, wait
hace calor—it's hot
hacer—make, do
hasta—until
hermano—brother
hora—time, hour
horario—schedule
jueves—Thursday
lejos—far
llegar, el—arrive
lugar—place
mamá—mother
mañana—morning
maravillosas—marvelous
mirar—look
Navidad—Christmas
necesitar—need
norte, el—north
papá—father
para—to, in order to
pasar—pass, spend (time)
playa—beach

poder—be able, can
¿por qué?—why?
porque—because
posible—possible
salir—leave
Santiago—capital of Chile
sábado—Saturday
semana—week
si—if
sorprenderse—be surprised
suerte, la—luck
tarde, la—afternoon
tiempo—time
tíos—aunt and uncle
todo—all
trabajar—work
último—last
vacaciones—vacation
veces—times
vienen: venir—come
viernes—Friday
Viña del Mar—city in
  Chile
vivir—live

45 El treinta de julio

Preguntas antes de leer:

1. ¿Cómo te sientes después de viajar por muchas horas?
2. ¿Cuáles son las primeras cosas que te gustaría hacer al llegar a un hotel nuevo?

Preguntas después de leer:

1. Cuando hace frío en el norte de los Estados Unidos, ¿qué tiempo hace en Paraguay? Cuando hace calor en los Estados Unidos, ¿qué tiempo hace en Argentina?
2. ¿En qué estación viajan estas norteamericanas? ¿Estás segura de que ésta es la estación correcta?
3. ¿Qué características debe tener un buen hotel? ¿Son necesarias todas estas cosas?

Notas culturales:

1. See also Chapter 28, *Es invierno, ¿sabes?* in this volume.
2. Asunción is the capital of Paraguay. Iguazú is the name of the longest (horizontal) waterfall in the world, which is located at the juncture of Paraguay, Argentina, and Brazil.

Otras actividades:

1. Ask students to check the international weather list in the newspaper or to watch a cable weather channel. Have them bring a weather report for a different part of the world.
2. You might want to ask students to check the weather for July and the weather for December in a number of vacation sites in the Hispanic world (San Juan, Caracas, Viña del Mar in Chile, Acapulco, Madrid, Costa del Sol). Also have them locate these sites on a map. Then ask them to decide if it would be better to visit there during their winter vacation, spring vacation, or summer vacation.
3. Ask students to describe the weather during a particular vacation period. (If they don't know the past tense well enough, let them do it in the narrative present.).
4. Have students study the Celsius or centigrade system. Is 32°C. cold? Is 20°C. a hot temperature, a nice temperature, or a cold temperature?

Suggestions for review:

Grammar review: use of infinitive after verbs *(querer, deber, parecer, poder); tener* expressions; verb phrases *(tener ganas de, ir a, alegrarse de);* and prepositions *(a, al, de)*
Vocabulary review: weather expressions; dates; days of week

Vocabulary

Vocabulario en adelante:

viajeras—travelers
joyería—jewelry store

encaje, el—lace
pulsera—bracelet

dije, el—charm
suerte, la—luck

Additional vocabulary—El tiempo:

hace frío—it's cold
hace sol—it's sunny
está lloviendo—it's raining
hay neblina—it's foggy
rayos, relámpagos—
  lightning

hace viento—it's windy
está nublado—it's cloudy
está nevando—it's snowing
hay una tempestad—it's
  stormy

hace fresco—it's cool
hay un arco iris—there's
  a rainbow
trueno—thunder

Pequeño diccionario:

agosto—August
agua, el—water
alegrarse—be happy
algo—something
allí—there
aquí—here
autobús, el—bus
bonito, bonita—pretty
buena—good
calendario—calendar
calor—heat
cansada—tired
chicas—girls
ciudad—city
comprar—buy
compras—shopping
creer—think, believe
cuándo—when
deber—should, ought to
dicen: decir—say, tell
dije, el—charm
día—day
dónde—where
ejercicio—exercise
encaje, el—lace
ganas—desire
haber—have (auxiliary)
hace calor—it's hot

hacer—do
hoy—today
interesantes—interesting
ir de compras—go
  shopping
itinerario—itinerary
joyería—jewelry, jewelry
  store
llamarse—be called
llegar—arrive
llevar—wear
magnífico—great,
  magnificent
mala—bad
más tarde—later
miércoles—Wednesday
mirar—look, look at
mujeres—women
nadar—swim
necesitar—need
noche, la—night
ñandutí—Paraguayan lace
otra—another
para—for
parecer—seem
piscina—swimming pool
poncho—heavy slit shawl
por—for

por fin—finally
¿por qué?—why?
posiblemente—possibly
primero—first
puede: poder—can, be able
  to
pulsera—bracelet
raro—strange
salir—leave
sábado—Saturday
según—according to
semana—week
sé: saber—know
si—if
suerte, la—luck
suéteres, los—sweaters
tanto—so much
temporaria—temporary
tener calor—to be hot
tener ganas—to be eager
tiempo—time, weather
tiendas—stores
todavía—still
un poco—a little
ver—see
viaje: de viaje—traveling
viajeras—travelers
yo también—me too

46   Las invitaciones están listas

Preguntas en adelante:

1. ¿Cuántas personas invitan a ustedes a una fiesta de cumpleaños normalmente?
2. ¿Escribes invitaciones formales?

Preguntas después de leer:

1. ¿Cómo invitas a las personas a una fiesta?
2. Cuando escribes invitaciones, ¿cómo las repartes?
3. ¿Qué mandas por correo? ¿tarjetas? ¿regalos?

Notas culturales:

1. The kind of invitations that we buy and fill in are very uncommon in Latin America, since they are also considered impersonal and, therefore, not courteous. Handwritten invitations must be delivered to the person face-to-face. They are not left in the mailbox, and are not given to a maid. One must talk to the person invited, and must not seem to be in a big hurry to leave and deliver more invitations.

2. The *quinceañera* is a Latin American custom. It is a girl's 15th birthday party and formally marks her transition from being a girl to being a young woman. She can date (although not with the freedom of many teenagers in the United States), she can wear formal dresses to big dances or parties, and she is called *señorita*.

Otras actividades:

1. Ask students to write personal invitations to their own birthday party—one to a neighbor, one to a family member, and a third to a close friend. Will everyone be told the same thing?

2. Suggest that any stamp collectors in class bring in examples of stamps from Hispanic countries.   You might want to go to a stamp dealer, since stamps often have interesting historical or cultural information, such as sketches of famous leaders, local flora and fauna, or famous buildings.

Suggestions for review:

Grammar review: direct versus indirect object pronouns
Vocabulary review: postal vocabulary

Vocabulary

Vocabulario para repasar en adelante:

quinceañera—15th birthday
correo—post office
edificio—building

repartir—deliver
pido: pedir—ask
entregar—deliver

bolsa—purse
llevar—take

Additional vocabulary: El correo

apartado postal—post office box
dirección—address
paquete, el—package
estampilla (timbre, sello)—stamp

buzón, el—mailbox
cartero, cartera—postal carrier
sobre, el—envelope
formulario—form

caja—box
correo aéreo—air mail
entrega urgente—special delivery
ventanilla—window

Pequeño diccionario:

agencia—agency
alegrarse—be glad
bolsa—purse
bolsita—small purse
bonita—pretty
carta—letter
casa—house
cámara—camera
claro—certainly
comer—eat
comprar—buy
con—with
conmigo—with me
correo—post office
creer—think, believe
cuando—when
después de—after
edificio—building
empezar—begin
enfrente de—facing, in front of
entregar—deliver
esperar—wait

familia—family
favor: por favor—please
fiesta—party
fotos, las—photos
gusto—pleasure
ha, hayas: haber—have
hora—time
invitación—invitation
lado: al lado de—next to
lista—ready
llamar—call
llegar—arrive
llevar—take
magnífica—great
necesitar—need
padres—parents
para—for, to, in order to
pasar—spend (time)
película—film
pido: pedir—ask
pienso en: pensar—plan
poder—can, be able
por favor—please

¿por qué?—why?
primero—first
problema, el—problem
puede: poder—can, be able to
quinceañera—fifteenth birthday
repartir—deliver
rollo—roll
salido—left
salir—leave
sea: ser—be (is)
señores—Mr. and Mrs.
tarde, la—afternoon
terminar—finish
tiempo—time
tienda—store
todas—all
todavía—yet
trabajar—work
ven: venir—come
ver—see
verano—summer

47 Garrapatos

Preguntas en adelante:

1. ¿Conoces a un agente de viajes? ¿Qué viajes recomienda esta persona?
2. Si le escribieras a un estudiante de otro país, ¿qué lugares en los Estados Unidos le recomendarías que visitara? ¿Qué lugares le recomendarías en tu estado o tu ciudad?
3. ¿Escribes bien? ¿Es fácil leer lo que escribes?

Preguntas después de leer:

1. ¿Es distinta tu firma? ¿Cómo?
2. ¿A quién conoces que tiene una firma no reconocible? ¿Cómo la reconoces entonces?

Notas culturales:

1. The verb "to scribble" is *garrapatear,* and the noun is *garrapatos,* very similar to the English expression "chicken scratches." Alternate forms are *garabatear* and *garabatos.*
2. *Iguazú* in the indigenous Guaraní language of the region, means "great water." These falls are higher than Niagara Falls and more than three times the length of the Horseshoe Falls. Actually, there are numerous falls, with the largest called "Devil's Throat." There are a number of new, modern, and luxurious hotels in the area.
3. Bariloche is in a Swiss-like area of Argentina with rugged mountains, lakes, national parks, extensive wildlife, and all kinds of sports and activities: mountain climbing, hiking, golf, swimming, fishing, hunting, camping, shopping, and in the wintertime skiing and ice skating.
4. The pampas extend like a fan around Buenos Aires for a distance of over 300 miles. The land is flat and treeless, except for eucalyptus avenues planted around the *estancias.* The cattle, wheat, and grains of the Pampas are products upon which Argentina depends economically.

Otras actividades:

1. You might suggest that students look at the signatures on dollar bills or the signatures of various presidents. Some, of course, are more legible than others. Or you might collect various hard-to-read signatures and let students try to guess whose signature it is.
2. Have students design and practice writing their own *rúbrica.* Then allow them a few minutes to write short notes to each other (be sure everyone both sends and gets notes), signed with their *rúbricas.* Or you might want everyone to write a general

note signed with their *rúbrica,* and then collect and post them. Let students try to match the *rúbrica* with the real name.

Suggestions for review:

Grammar review: future; conditional; subjunctive
Vocabulary review: geographical terms

Vocabulary

Vocabulario para repasar en adelante:

sugerirías—would suggest
parece—seem like
frontera—border
este—east
arreglar—arrange
hospedaje, el—lodging
firma—signature

país, el—country
gauchos—Argentinian
  cowboys
pedir—ask
paisaje, el—countryside
huéspedes—guests
garrapatos—scribbles

tener razón—be correct
vaqueros—cowboys
cataratas, las—waterfall
agradar—be grateful,
  thankful
carta de presentación—
  letter of introduction

Additional vocabulary—El mapa:

altiplano—high plain
continente, el—continent
estrecho—strait
llano—plain
península—peninsula
selva—forest

bahía—bay
cordillera—mountain chain
isla—island
océano—ocean
playa—beach

barranca—ravine
desierto—desert
istmo—isthmus
pantano—swamp
río—river

Pequeño diccionario:

agente—agent
agradar—be grateful,
  thankful
algunas—some
allí—there
amigo—friend
Andes, los—mountains in
  South America
aquí—here
arreglar—arrange
así—thus, that way
autobús, el—bus
Bariloche—city in the
  Andes
bastante—enough
Brasil—Brazil
bueno—good

carta—letter
casa—house
cataratas, las—waterfalls
como—like
conocer—know, meet
costar—cost
costo—cost
cuanto: en cuanto al—
  concerning
cuesta: costar—cost
dejar—let, allow
deportes, los—sports
después—after
dicen: decir—say
diferencias—differences
diferentes—different
dinero—money

ejemplo—example
entre—between
esquiar—ski
Estados Unidos—United
  States
este, el—east
firma—signature
frontera—border
garrapatos—scribbles
gauchos—Argentinian
  cowboys
gente, la—people
grande—big
gusto—pleasure
hermano—brother
hospedaje, el—lodging
huéspedes, los—guests

igualmente—same
Iguazú—waterfalls in
  northeastern Argentina
importar—be important
impresionante—impressive
interesante—interesting
interés—interest
invierno—winter
lagos—lakes
leer—read
letra—letter
llamarse—be named
lugar, el—place
magnífico—great
mamá—mother
mapa, el—map
médico—doctor
mirar—look
muchísimas—very many
nada—nothing
ninguna—not any, none
nombre, el—name

oeste, el—west
ofrezcan: ofrecer—offer
ojalá—I hope
oportunidad—opportunity
otro—another
país, el—country
pampas—plains
para—for, to, in order to
parecer—seem like
pequeño—small
pido: pedir—ask
por—for, through
porque—because
posible—possible
posiblemente—possibly
presentación—introduction
presentar—introduce
problema—problem
recomendación—
  recommendation
recomendar—recommend
reconocer—recognize
reconocible—recognizable

reducido—reduced
seguro—sure
si—if
siento: lo siento—I'm sorry
sugerir—suggest
también—also
tendré: tener—have
tengas: tener razón—be
  right
tío—uncle
toda—all
todo—everything
transporte, el—
  transportation
vaqueros—cowboys
ver—see
verano—summertime
vez: a la vez—at the same
  time
viajar—travel
viaje, el—trip
visitar—visit

48 ¿Quihúbole?

Preguntas en adelante:

1. ¿Sabes hablar más de una lengua?
2. ¿Conoces a una persona que es difícil de entender?

Preguntas después de leer:

1. ¿Cuáles son algunas diferencias del inglés de varias partes de los Estados Unidos?
2. ¿Qué palabras hay en inglés que solamente usan los jóvenes?
3. ¿Haces o vas a fiestas grandes o pequeñas? ¿Qué te gusta hacer en las fiestas?
4. ¿Dónde haces o vas a fiestas?

Notas culturales:

1. See the additional cultural information in Answer A and Answer C.
2. See Chapter 11, *El regalo,* and Chapter 20, *Reina,* in this volume.
3. *Chucha* is a nickname for María Jesús, and *Goyo* for Gregorio.
4. You might want students to differentiate slang, formal and informal language, idiomatic language, and dialects and regional variations in order to become more aware of language differences. Slang consists of usually short-lived words and expressions of a particular age group, period of time, or event. Examples are "twenty-three skidoo" and "Where's the beef?" Formal language such as "Good evening. How do you do?" is used in formal situations. Informal language like "Hi, how's it goin'?" is used with family, friends, and in this country, among young peers. Idioms are expressions whose real meaning does not match their surface meaning: "the cat's got her tongue," for example, or "jump for joy." Dialects are legitimate regional variations within a language. Boston English differs from a Southern drawl. Some parts of the country say "soda" for a soft drink and others say "pop."

Otras actividades:

1. Have students list slang expressions and idiomatic expressions in English. Then decide how these might be expressed in standard Spanish.
2. Ask students in small groups of three or four to write another "Mexican" conversation. Then have them perform it in front of the class. Give a prize for the best performance.

Suggestions for review:

Grammar review: uses of the verb *ir*
Vocabulary review: idiomatic expressions

Vocabulary

Vocabulario para repasar en adelante:

(Because the focus of this capsule is unknown vocabulary, you may not want to present the vocabulary in advance.)

pachanga—party
cuates—friends
platicar—talk, chat
¡Híjole—Wow!
en onda—"with it"
elepés, los—LPs, records
plata—silver: coins
compadre—close friend, relationship between a parent and a godparent

alberca—swimming pool
diablal, el—large group
chamacas—girls
viejos—"old" married people
chau—so long
gringo—American

balneario—swiming resort
¿Quihúbole—What's up?
lunada—evening party
mero—very, exact
brincos dieras—don't you wish
feria—small amount of money, coins

Additional vocabualry:

ahí no más—right here, within reach
hacer chorcha—get together with friends for a while
'Horita vengo—I'm coming!
nadita—absolutamente nada.
pochismo—Mexican Spanish corrupted by American English
¡Qué horitas!—It's about time!

¡Frijoles!—expression of annoyance or disgust
hacer ojitos—flirt
Igualito—absolutely equal or the same.
Ni modo—No way.
¡Anímate! ¡Orale—Come on!
¡Qué diablitos!—What the ..!!!
¡Chócala!—Expression of good intent in offering to shake hands, give a "high five," or to clink glasses as in a toast.

Pequeño diccionario:

además—besides
ahí—here
Ahí nos vemos—See you later.
alberca—swimming pool
ándale—polite expression giving someone permission to leave
apartamento—apartment
aquí mero—right here
balneario—simming resort
baño: traje de baño, el—bathing suit
Brincos dieras—Don't you wish?
cerca de—close to

chamacas: muchachas—girls
chau—so long
compadre—very close friend
cuates—close friends
diablal, el—large group
dieras: brincos dieras—don't you wish?
divertirse—enjoy oneself
domingo—Sunday
dónde—where
elepés, los—LPs, records
enorme—huge
entiendo:entender—understand

feria—small amount of money; coins
fin de semana—weekend
gringo—American
habrá—will there be
¡Híjole!—Wow!
hola—hi
jóvenes—young people
llevar—take, wear
lunada—outdoor evening party
'mano: hermano—brother, good friend
mariachi, los—Mexican musical group
mero—very, exact

mirar—look
mundo: todo el mundo—
  everyone
nada—nothing, not
  anything
nadar—swim
ni .. ni—neither ... nor
noticias, las—news
nuevo—new
onda: en onda—with it, on
  the wave
pachanga—party
padre—nice, great,
  marvelous

planear—plan
plata—silver, coins
platicar—chat, talk
pos: pues—well
próxima—next
Puebla—city southeast of
  Mexico City
quiénes—who all
**¿quihúbole?: hola, ¿qué
  tal?**—Hi, what's up?
sábado—Saturday
semana—week
simón—a big yes
Teotihuacán—area and
  town near pyramids

Tlalpan—area of Mexico
  City
todo el mundo—everyone
todos—all
traje de baño, el—bathing
  suit
vacaciones, las—vacation
vámonos—Let's go
viejos—old: in this case
  "old" married people
viene: venir—come
viernes—Friday
volcán, el—volcano

49 El desfile

Preguntas en adelante:

1. ¿Qué te gusta ver cuando vas a los desfiles?
2. ¿Cuándo hay desfiles en los Estados Unidos?

Preguntas después de leer:

1. ¿Qué hacen las iglesias cristianas de los Estados Unidos durante la semana antes de la Pascua Florida?
2. ¿Celebran ustedes (tú y tu familia) la Pascua Florida? Si la celebran, ¿qué hacen? Si no, ¿qué fiesta que se celebra en tu familia te gusta más?

Notas culturales

1. These religious parades are held the week before Easter in all Spanish-speaking countries, although the dress of the people in the parades differs from country to country. All have religious floats depicting the life of Christ, and all parades have candles and flowers, either on the floats or carried by marchers. In some places, elaborate carpets of floral leaves or colored sand are laid along the parade route. In Spain, Seville has especially elaborate processions, and in Mexico, the processions of Taxco are considered the most spectacular.
2. Another area of possible misunderstanding for non-Hispanics is the use of the terms *negrito* or *negrita*. Because of their endings, the words have a positive connotation. When *negrita* is used as a *piropo*, for example, to describe a young girl, it would carry the connotation of "cute" or "pretty". Both the masculine and feminine forms are commonly employed as pet names.

Otras actividades

1. In pairs, have students take turns naming holiday activities. The partner not doing the naming tries to guess the holiday.
2. You might want to suggest that students ask someone older than 50 how the observation of Easter, or another holiday, has changed during their lifetime.

Suggestions for review:

Grammar review: uses of *por* (*¿por qué? por eso, por supuesto, gracias por, por ahí, tenemos respeto por*)
Vocabulary review: holidays; parades (*desfile, carroza, globos, banda, marchar, etc.*)

Vocabulary

Vocabulario para repasar en adelante:

desfile, el—parade
estrenar—wear for the first time
carroza—float
miedo—fear

Pascua Florida—Easter
nadie—no one
callado—quiet
gritar—shout

verdadero—true
animado—animated, lively
Redentor, el—Redeemer
cofradía—religious society

Additional vocabulary: Días de fiesta

Día de Brujas—Halloween
Día de los Enamorados—Valentine's Day
Día de Reyes—Three Kings' Day, Jan. 6
Miércoles de cenizas—Ash Wednesday
Nochebuena—Christmas Eve
Víspera del Año Nuevo, Noche Vieja—New Year's Eve

Día de los Difuntos—Day of the Dead, Nov. 2
Domingo de Ramos—Palm Sunday
Navidad, Navidades—Christmas
Viernes Santo—Good Friday

Pequeño diccionario

abuela—grandmother
afroamericana—African-American
ahí—there
ahora—now
animado—animated, lively
antes—before
aquí—here
así—that way
azul—blue
bandas—bands
bonitas—pretty
¡bravo!—rah! yay!
callado—quiet
carroza—float
centro—center, downtown
clase, la—kind
cofradía—religious society
creer—think, believe
de veras—really
desfile, el—parade
disculpar—pardon, excuse
esta noche—tonight
Estados Unidos—United States
estrenar—wear for the first time

estudiante—student
estupendas—great
exactamente—exactly
flores, las—flowers
gritar—shout
grupo—group
invitar—invite
llamar—call
lo que—what
luces, las—lights
más tarde—later
miedo—fear
mirar—look
mucho—much, a lot of
mujeres—women
nadie—no one
ninguna—not any, nothing
noche, la—night
nombre, el—name
nueva—new
ocasión—occasion
otro—another
para—in order to
parecer—seem
parte, la—part
Pascua Florida—Easter
paseo—walk
por—for, towards

por ahí—over there
por eso—that's why
¿por qué?—why?
por supuesto—of course
procesiones—processions
puedo: poder—can, be able to
realmente—really
Redentor, el—Redeemer
respeto—respect
rojo—red
ropa, la—clothes
sea: ser—be (am, is, are)
Semana Santa—Holy Week
seria—serious
si—if
sociedad—society
sol, el—sun
tampoco—neither, either
tan—so
tener miedo—be afraid
tío—uncle
todos—all
ver—see
verdadero—real, true
viene: venir—come

50 Uy, ¡qué horrible!

Preguntas en adelante:

1. ¿Dónde está el cementerio más cercano? ¿Cómo es?
2. ¿Cuándo vamos al cementerio?

Preguntas después de leer:

1. En tu opinión o según tu religión, ¿qué le pasa al espíritu después de la muerte? ¿Se queda con el cuerpo? ¿Va al cielo? ¿Se reencarna?
2. Es muy importante que haya una cantidad suficiente de órganos para la transplantación. ¿Cuál es tu opinión sobre el uso del cuerpo después de la muerte?

Notas culturales:

1. Note that there are two correct answers in this section: B and D.
2. In Guanajuato, Mexico, the sandy dry soil has created numerous mummies, which are on display in a museum. Additionally, there are bones and mummies of the early indigenous populations on display in the Museum of Anthropology in Mexico City, and elsewhere.
3. In Cuba after a number of years, the bones are dug up and placed in a much smaller compartment.
4. An American's best course of action when someone dies is to say only *Mi más sentido pésame.* Rather than trying to look at the positive side as many Americans do, Mexicans look at the tragic side, allowing the bereaved to rise heroically above the tragedy.

Otras actividades:

1. You may want students to write figures of speech about death (human, animal, plant), such as similes, metaphors, etc.
2. You may want older students to read one of the short stories about death that abound in Spanish literature such as *Chac Mool,* by Carlos Fuentes;

Suggestions for review:

Grammar review *hacer* + time + que; conditional; past subjunctive recognition
Vocabulary review: death vocabulary (*cementerio, mausoleo,* etc.)

Vocabulary

Vocabulario para repasar en adelante:

murió: morir—die
has dicho—you have told
tierra santa—holy ground
huesos—bones
dejarlos—leave them
fue, fuera: ser—be (was, were)

quisieras: querer—want
haber sido—have been
pudiéramos: poder—can, be able to
deprimido—depressing
guerra—war

lápida—gravestone
piedra—stone
muralla—wall
desenterrados—unearthed, dug up

Additional vocabulary—La muerte:

cadáver, el—cadaver, dead body
fúnebre—funereal
solemne—solemn
vivo—alive

enterrar—bury
cielos—heaven
muerte, la—death
pésames, los—condolences

funerario—funeral
funeraría—funeral home
muerto—dead
tumba—tomb, grave

Pequeño diccionario:

abuelita—grandmother
abuelo, abuelito—grandfather
aceptar—accept
acompañar—accompany
alegrarse—be glad
allí—there
años—years
aquí—here
bastante—enough
cementerio—cemetery
como—as
comprar—buy
conmigo—with me
conociera: conocer—know
deber—ought to, must
dejar—leave
deprimido—depressing
desenterrados—unearthed, dug up
después de—after
dicho: decir—tell
enseñar—show, teach
exactamente—exactly
familia—family

flores, las—flowers
fue, fuera: ser—be (was, were)
gente, la—people
grande—big
guerra—war
haber—have
hace muchos años—many years ago
has: haber—have
huesos—bones
lado—side
lápida—gravestone
lástima—shame
llevar—take
lugar, el—room
mirar—buy
montón—mountain, pile
muchacha—girl
muchísimas—many, many
muralla—wall
murió: morir—die
nada más—that's all
ochenta y seis—86
para—to

parecer—seem
persona—person
piedra—stone
pobres—poor, poor things
poca—little
poner—put, place
por—because
por eso—that's why
posible—possible
pudiéramos: poder—can, be able to
quisieras: querer—want
remedios—remedies, alternatives
santa—holy
si—if
sido: ser—be
simpática—nice
sobre—about
tan—as
tierra—land, ground
tierra santa—holy ground
varios—several
ya—already

51 Un buen partido

Preguntas en adelante:

1. ¿Qué actividades hay en los parques los domingos en la tarde?
2. ¿Qué hacen tú y tu familia o tus amigos los domingos en la tarde?

Preguntas después de leer:

1. ¿Cuáles son los símbolos de los partidos políticos en los Estados Unidos?
2. Además de los equipos deportivos, ¿qué cosas tienen un color específico?

Notas culturales:

1. Note that the *Caribe* team and the *Partido de Acción Social Americana* are both fictional.
2. See Chapter 52, *Vote por los verdes*, and Chapter 53, *El mejor candidato,* in this volume.
3. In the United States, political apathy among young voters is endemic, but in other countries, it is the young voters who are often the most active and ardent advocates of a political party. Most major universities are "safe havens" for those opposed to the ruling party. Many young people participate in demonstrations, work on student newsletters, and discuss politics for hours on end. Most of these young people are truly interested in working toward a better life for the people in their country, and they see politics as a way to accomplish their objectives.
4. A number of European countries, including Spain, have "green" parties that promote environmentalism and oppose nuclear weapons.

Otras actividades:

1. You might want to have students collect newspaper and magazine articles about the political process in Hispanic countries. Additionally, they can use the library for information and/or interview people (such as former Peace Corps workers, local politicians with an interest in a specific country, and people who do business with or in another country). Let individual students choose from the countries that are currently in the news, give them a month to collect information, and then have a report day.
2. If there are elections near at hand, have students write political statements representative of the party of their choice, and then have a partner guess which party they are describing.

Suggestions for review:

Grammar review: comparatives; compound sentences with *creer que, suponer que, decir que, (es) claro que*
Vocabulary review: political vocabulary

Vocabulary

Vocabulario para repasar en adelante:

me gustaría—I'd like to
anotar—score
supongo: suponer—suppose
proponen: proponer—propose
jefa—head, chief

asistir—attend
partidario—follower, supporter
discurso—speech
banderas—flags
escoger—choose

gente, la—people
portero—goalie
tierra—earth
mejorar—improve
por lo menos—at least
cambiar—change

Additional vocabulary—La política:

alcalde, alcaldesa—mayor
liberal—liberal
político—politician
funcionario—lower-level official
legislatura—legislature

caudillo—political leader
congreso—Congress
senador—senator
comité, el—committee
independiente—independent
ley, la—law

legislador—legislator
conservador—conservative
contribuyente—taxpayer
elección—election
representante—representative

Pequeño diccionario:

acción—action
allí—there
amarilla—yellow
americana—American
anotar—score
año—year
aquí—here
asistir—attend
aunque—although
ayudan: ayudar—help
azul—blue
banderas—flags
blanca—white
cambiar—change
camiseta—tee shirt
candidatos—candidates
claro—certainly
comité, el—committee
comprehensivo—comprehensive, complete

correr—run
creer—think, believe
cuándo—when
deber—ought to, should
decidir—decide
dicen: decir—say
discurso—speech
domingo—Sunday
economía—economy
educación—education
elecciones—elections
entiendes: entender—understand
equipo—team
escoger—choose
escuchar—listen to
estado—state
futbolista—football player
ganar—win
gente, la—people

gobernador—governor
goles, los—goals
gran—great
gustaría—would like
hacer—do
hermana—sister
hoy—today
importancia—importance
importantes—important
jefa—chief, head
jóvenes—young people
listo—ready
llevar—wear
maravillosa—marvelous, great
mejor—better, best
mejorar—improve
nada más que—anything but
negra—black

otro—another
para—for, in order to
parecer—seem
parque, el—park
partidario—follower, supporter, partisan
partido—game, political party
pasar—pass
plataforma—platform
político—political
por lo menos—at least

portero—goalie
primera—first, primary
programa—program
proponer—propose
razón: tener razón—be right
República Dominicana—Dominican Republic
responsabilidad—responsibility
reunión—meeting, rally
ropa, la—clothes
salir—leave

salvación—salvation
Santo Domingo—capital of the Dominican Republic
supongo que sí—I suppose so
también—also
tan pronto como—as soon as
tarde, la—afternoon
tierra—earth
ver—see
verde—green
zapatos—shoes

52 Vote por los verdes

Preguntas en adelante:

1. En las próximas elecciones, ¿hay candidatos para quienes quieres votar? ¿Por qué?
2. ¿Ayudas en algunas elecciones? ¿en la escuela, en la ciudad, o en el estado?
3. ¿Hay causas importantes que apoyas?

Preguntas después de leer:

1. ¿Cuáles son las ventajas y desventajas de votar por candidatos de un solo partido político aquí en los Estados Unidos?
2. ¿Qué otros sistemas de votar conoces? Descríbelos un poco.

Notas culturales:

1. See the additional cultural information in Answer A and Answer C.
2. See *Un buen partido,* Chapter 51, and *El mejor candidato,* Chapter 53, in this volume.
3. *En ocho días* means "in a week."
4. Venezuela has more than 30 political parties, so there are many coalitions of parties.

Otras actividades:

1. You might want to ask students to report on the government of one of the Hispanic countries.
2. Ask students to write statements that describe the two major American political parties. Then have them work in pairs reading their statements to each other. The other student can guess which political party is being described.

Suggestions for review:

Grammar review: prepositions; conditional; present subjunctive
Vocabulary review: election vocabulary

Vocabulary

Vocabulario para repasar en adelante:

pegar—paste, post
cada—each
encuestas—surveys
promover—promote
calificaciones—
    qualifications

carteles, los—posters
adelantados—ahead
nos esforzamos más—
    we try harder
vale—it's worth

diseminar—disseminate,
    spread
parecer—seem
merecer—deserve

Additional vocabulary—Las elecciones:

balota—ballot
ciudadano—citizen
convención—convention
demócrata—Democrat
partidario—party member
lugar de votación—polling place

registro electoral—registration
constitución—constitution
democracia—democracy
elección preliminar—primary election
republicano—Republican
campaña—campaign

Pequeño diccionario:

ahora—now
alegrarse—be glad
amigo—friend
antes de—before
aquí—here
ayudar—help
bastante—enough
cada—each
calificación—qualification
candidato, candidata—
  candidate
carteles, los—posters
cine, el—movies
claro—of course
con—with
conmigo—with me
conociste: conocer—meet
contigo—with you
creer—think, believe
cuál—which
cuándo—when
después de—after
diseminar—disseminate,
  spread
días, los—days
elecciones—election
encuestas—surveys, polls
escuelas—schools
esforzarse—try

estudiante—student
fantástico—fantastic
ganar—win
hacer—do
importante—important
importar—be important
informes, los—information
invitar—invite
lista—list
mayor—greater
menos—except
merecer—deserve
necesario—necessary
necesitar—need
ninguna—none, not any
noche, la—night
número—numbers
para—for, to in order to
parecer—seem
partido—party
pegar—paste, put up
pensar—plan
por—throughout, for
por eso—that's why
¿por qué?—why?
posición—position
primera—first
problema, el—problem
prometer—promise

promover—promote
puedo, puede: poder—can,
  to be able to
quedar—remain
saber—know
salgan: salir—come out
seguro, segura—sure
según—according to
senador—senator
sería: ser—be
si—if
significar—mean
tendrá: tener—have
terceros, los—thirds
tiempo—time
todas, todos—all, everyone
todavía—yet
universidades—universities
valer—be worth
vayan: ir—go
vente: venir—come
verdad—true
verdes—green
vez: en vez de—instead of
votante—voter
votar—vote
voto—vote
ya—already

53 El mejor candidato

Preguntas en adelante:

1. ¿Crees que es importante la política?
2. ¿Cómo aprendemos de los candidatos en los Estados Unidos? ¿Miras las convenciones en la televisión? ¿Escuchas los discursos de los candidatos?

Preguntas después de leer:

1. ¿Cuáles son las características que deben tener los candidatos políticos en los Estados Unidos?
2. ¿Qué profesión o empleo tenían varios políticos en los Estados Unidos antes de llegar a ser políticos? Menciona el nombre, su cargo y su profesión anterior.

Notas culturales:

1. Note that the candidates are fictional.
2. See the additional cultual information in Answer C and Answer D.
3. See Chapter 51, *Un buen partido,* and Chapter 52, *Vote por los verdes,* in this volume.
4. Note that the topic here is the candidate for election, not the politicians themselves. More generals have become leaders of their countries than those of any other profession. However, the majority are not elected but rather seize power through an overthrow of the government. Famous scholar/leaders in the past have included Luis Muñoz Marín of Puerto Rico and José Martí of Cuba, for example.

Otras actividades:

1. You might want to have students do reports on famous author/scholars who were also politically active in their countries.
2. First, have students make a list of characteristics that candidates should have. Then rank them in the following order: 1) what characteristics *should* candidates have, and 2) what characteristics *do* they have?
3. Have students design a poster for a political candidate from a Hispanic country (imaginary or real).

Suggestions for review:

Grammar review: *gustar*-type verbs *(aburrir, interesar, faltar);* subjunctive with impersonal expressions
Vocabulary review: things to read; education vocabulary

Vocabulary

Vocabulario para repasar en adelante:

aburre: aburrir—bore
vida—life
explica—explain
horario—schedule
país, el—country

negocios, los—business
falta—lacks
mejorar—improve
entrevista—interview
andina—Andean (from
    Andes Mountains)

estar de acuerdo—agree
ensayos—essays
pobreza—poverty
ganar—win

Additional vocabulary: Para leer:

historietas cómicas—comic books
artículo—article
ciencia ficción—science fiction
misterio—mystery
cuentos cortos—short stories
revistas—magazines
fotonovelas—photo story magazine
informe, el—report

periódico—newspaper
carta—letter
literatura—literature
novela—novel
enciclopedia—encyclopedia
drama, el—play
biografías—biographies
poemas—poems

Pequeño diccionario:

aburrir—bore
acompañarme—accompany
  me
acuerdo: estar de
  acuerdo—agree
además—besides, also
algún—some
andina—Andean
aquí—here
buscar—look for
candidato—candidate
clase, la—class
colecciones—collections
comprar—buy
con—with
contiene: contener—contain
creer—think, believe
día, el—day
economía—economy
educación—education
elecciones—elections
empieza: empezar—begin
ensayos—essays

entiende: entender—
  understand
entrevista—interview
especialista—specialist
esta noche—tonight
estado—state
estudiar—study
exacta—exact
examen, el—exam
experiencia—experience
explicar—explain
exportaciones, las—exports
faltar—lack
fue: ser—be (was)
futuro—future
fútbol—soccer
gane, ganó: ganar—win
hablar—talk, speak
hora—time
horario—schedule
hoy—today
importante—important
indicar—indicate

inteligentes—intelligent
interesar—interest
joven—young
legislatura—legislature
libros—books
literatura—literature
mañana—tomorrow
mejor—better, best
mejorar—improve
mirar—watch
montón, el—pile, large
  quantitiy
nacional—national
negocios, los—business
norteamericano—American
  (US)
novela—novel
obvio—obvious
país, el—country
para—for
partido—game
pasado mañana—day after
  tomorrow

Thematic Units

The following groupings are suggestions for possible thematic units.

Names

		Topics
2.	**Bienvenidos**	First names in the United States
3.	**Es de Venezuela**	Ethnic names
4.	**¿Qué le llaman al bebé?**	Second last name
5.	**Amigos, primos y novios**	Popular names
47.	**Garrapatos**	*Rúbricas*

Courtesy

1.	**A sus órdenes**	Polite introductions
6.	**Don Javier**	Titles of address
7.	**Señor Licenciado**	Titles with *señor*, etc.
8.	**Hey, Mister**	Spanish vs. English forms of address
9.	**Sí, señorita**	*Señora* vs. *señorita*
35.	**¿Dónde está el Focolare?**	Display of courtesy
46.	**Las invitaciones están listas**	Hand-delivering invitations

School

12.	**Malas notas, malas noticias**	A grade of six (out of ten)
13.	**Escuelas por todas partes**	Secondary schools, colleges
14.	**El colegio**	*Colegio* versus college
15.	**El club**	No extracurricular activities
17.	**¿Qué llevas hoy?**	School uniforms

Food

21.	**Pido la pizza**	*Paella valenciana*
22.	**¡Cuánta comida!**	*Sopa seca*
23.	**Enchiladas verdes**	*Picante* versus *caliente*
27.	**¿Vamos a comer guisantes?**	Frozen foods in the United States

Meals

19. **Somos doce**	Large tables in restaurants
25. **La cena**	The evening meal
30. **El domingo**	A picnic in the country
31. **La cuenta, por favor**	Asking for the check
32. **La mesa al lado de la ventana**	Tablecloths

Social Customs

18. **La niñera**	Babysitters
24. **Voy al mercado**	Going to market daily
36. **No soy tu novia**	Standing too close
37. **Besos olvidados**	*Telenovelas*
39. **Es un buen precio**	*Amiguismo*–setting a price

.House and Home

26. **Es hora de comer**	Eating in the kitchen
42. **Nuestra casa**	The barrio
43. **Mi casa es tu casa**	High walls

Language

10. **Mi cachorro**	Animals vs. people
11. **El regalo**	*Pequeñez*
20. **Reina**	Diminutive endings, nicknames
48. **¿Quihúbole?**	Mexican Spanish

Time, Weather, Geography, Etc.

28. **Es invierno ¿sabes?**	Seasons
33. **La frontera**	Name variations (Rio Grande/Bravo)
44. **A las quince**	24-hour clock
45. **El treinta de julio**	"Winter" weather

Life's Major Events: Weddings, Celebrations and Funerals

16. **Las mañanitas**	Mariachis and serenades
29. **En San Cristóbal**	Town celebrating saint's day
38. **Las rosas sí**	Funeral flowers

40. **Las bodas de Angélica**	Two meanings of *madrina*
41. **Las madrinas**	What bridesmaids do
49. **El desfile**	Holy Week processions
50. **Uy, ¡qué horrible!**	Bones in cemetery

Politics

34. **Vamos a Puerto Rico**	No passport needed
51. **Un buen partido**	Political rallies in park
52. **Vote por los verdes**	A party names officials
53. **El mejor candidato**	Scholar-presidents

Additional Vocabulary Topics

1.	**A sus órdenes**	Courtesy expressions
2.	**Bienvenidos**	Hispanic nationalities
3.	**Es de Venezuela**	Nationalities
4.	**¿Qué le llaman al bebé?**	Ordinal numbers
5.	**Amigos, primos y novios**	Descriptions
6.	**Don Javier**	Jewelry
7.	**Señor Licenciado**	Employment
8.	**Hey, Mister!**	Clothes
9.	**Sí, señorita**	Family
10.	**Mi cachorro**	Animals
11.	**El regalo**	Presents
12.	**Malas notas, malas noticias**	Classes
13.	**Escuelas por todas partes**	Advanced classes
14.	**El colegio**	Time expressions
15.	**El club**	Sports
16.	**Las mañanitas**	Musical instruments
17.	**¿Qué llevas hoy?**	Reflexives
18.	**La niñera**	Feelings
19.	**Somos doce**	Clothes and colors
20.	**Reina**	Children
21.	**Pido la pizza**	Junk food
22.	**¡Cuánta comida!**	Food
23.	**Enchiladas verdes**	Food description
24.	**Voy al mercado**	Hispanic food
25.	**La cena**	Places to go
26.	**Es hora de comer**	Rooms of house
27.	**¿Vamos a comer guisantes?**	Food preparation
28.	**Es invierno, ¿sabes?**	Parts of body
29.	**En San Cristóbal**	Months
30.	**El domingo**	Picnic vocabulary
31.	**La cuenta, por favor**	Love and friendship
32.	**La mesa al lado de la ventana**	Table-setting

33. **La frontera**	Travel
34. **Vamos a Puerto Rico**	Days of week, seasons
35. **¿Dónde está el Focolare?**	Prepositions of location
36. **No soy tu novia**	Commands
37. **Besos olvidados**	Television and movies
38. **Las rosas, sí**	Stores
39. **Es un buen precio**	Shopping
40. **Las bodas de Angélica**	Weddings
41. **Las madrinas**	Positive adjectives
42. **Nuestra casa**	Adverbs (*-mente*)
43. **Mi casa es tu casa**	Outside the house
44. **A las quince**	Transportation
45. **El treinta de julio**	Weather
46. **Las invitaciones están listas**	Post office
47. **Garrapatos**	Geography
48. **¿Quihubole?**	Mexican expressions
49. **El desfile**	Holidays
50. **Uy, ¡qué horrible!**	Death
51. **Un buen partido**	Politics
52. **Vote por los verdes**	Elections
53. **El mejor candidato**	Things to read

Answer Key

1. D	28. C
2. A	29. B
3. C	30. D
4. B	31. A
5. B	32. A
6. A	33. C
7. D	34. B
8. D	35. D
9. C	36. A
10. D	37. C
11. A	38. C
12. C	39. C
13. D	40. A
14. A	41. B
15. B	42. A
16. B	43. C
17. C	44. D
18. D	45. A
19. B	46. B
20. C	47. D
21. B	48. D
22. A	49. C
23. D	50. B, D
24. A	51. A
25. B	52. D
26. C	53. B
27. B	

Notes

Notes

Notes